Coping with Tensions

Coping with Tensions

A Catalyst for Transformative Change for Teachers and Administrators

Chelsea Faase, Sheila Kohl, and Jason Lau

ROWMAN & LITTLEFIELD
Lanham • Boulder • New York • London

Published by Rowman & Littlefield
An imprint of The Rowman & Littlefield Publishing Group, Inc.
4501 Forbes Boulevard, Suite 200, Lanham, Maryland 20706
www.rowman.com

86-90 Paul Street, London EC2A 4NE

Copyright © 2022 by Chelsea Faase, Sheila Kohl, and Jason Lau

All rights reserved. No part of this book may be reproduced in any form or by any electronic or mechanical means, including information storage and retrieval systems, without written permission from the publisher, except by a reviewer who may quote passages in a review.

British Library Cataloguing in Publication Information Available

Library of Congress Cataloging-in-Publication Data Available

ISBN 9781475860771 (cloth) | ISBN 9781475860788 (pbk.) | ISBN 9781475860795 (ebook)

Contents

Foreword	vii
Acknowledgments	ix
Introduction	1
Chapter 1: Tensions in Schools	7
Chapter 2: Finding the Joy in Our Tensions	31
Chapter 3: When Organizational Tensions Affect Culture	45
Chapter 4: What We Wish Administrators Knew	61
Chapter 5: What We Wish Teachers Knew	75
Chapter 6: How Do We Take Care of Each Other?	89
Chapter 7: The Path of Enlightenment	103
Chapter 8: Now What?	117
Conclusion	131
Tables	137
About the Authors	139

Foreword

As members of the human race, we endeavor to manage tensions in all aspects of life. Most often we view these tensions as unwelcome annoyances and look for ways to avoid, ignore, or release those tensions. You may recall the *Seinfeld* episode in which the character Frank Costanza, played by Jerry Stiller, when faced with moments in which the authors have defined as tensions, looks heavenward, arms raised, and utters, "Serenity now!" Ah, that such a simple expression provided the remedy!

In *Coping with Tensions: A Catalyst for Transformative Change for Teachers and Administrators*, the authors create a tension by testing our conceptions of tension. The term *tension* likely conjures up a negative connotation. The authors challenge this by introducing us to and exploring the notion of positive tension.

While the authors concede that everyone experiences tension and works to navigate it, the intended audience for this volume is educators. Through adeptly using anecdotes, vignettes, and stories, *Coping with Tensions* serves to amplify the voices of educators in various roles, including teachers, principals, and superintendents. This book includes insights into the stressors and tensions identified by educators as themes emerge across roles. Noteworthy is the fact that, by examining the stressors within the school and district context, essential characteristics of a productive school culture are brought to the fore.

Coping with Tensions is practical, and the testimonials of the educators are relatable, each providing insights into the identified tension or stressor along with ways to both address and lean into that tension. Additionally, the authors cite relevant research to support not only the perspectives represented by educators but also the strategies and recommendations intended to improve our responses, provide relief, and increase our ability to cope.

Coping with Tensions results in the authors' challenge of the reader: namely, to not only embrace tensions but to find joy in them. They postulate that by acknowledging that tensions exist, by getting to the root cause, and by implementing tools and strategies, we can reframe our perceptions of tensions so they can serve as motivation to drive change in ourselves, in each other, and in our organizations. Finally, with each chapter the reader is encouraged to engage in the practice of reflection and perhaps a path to serenity—now.

Barbara J. Sramek, PhD
Retired Superintendent
Clinical Professor
Director, Wisconsin Idea Executive PhD Program
University of Wisconsin–Madison

Acknowledgments

CHELSEA

This book would not have been possible without the knowledge, experiences, and willingness to embrace the tensions of my co-authors, Jason and Sheila. You both are incredible educators who constantly work to be better, for yourself and for the educational environments that are so fortunate to have you. Thank you for doing this work, to better understand tensions, and to use these to continue to push education forward. Our roundtable discussions on tensions were one of my favorite parts of this process.

To my family, who continues to support and motivate me to reach for the stars in every new endeavor. Thank you for your gentle reminders on my deadlines, for the coffee deliveries, and quick check-ins. I am so fortunate to grow as a person and as an educator due to watching each of you every day. Whether teaching was your vocation or not, you are educators to everyone who is lucky enough to be around you. Thank you for the front row seat in how you are changing the world. Finally, and specifically, to my father. Growing up with a sociologist educator, a lover of people and life, positioned me for this book even before it was a possibility. I know he is smiling down on me, knowing that I am continuing his work.

SHEILA

First, thank you to Chelsea and Jason for suggesting such an outlandish idea as writing a book about the tensions educators face. It was truly a pleasure working with you to delve into the information gleaned from our interviews with educators. I learned as much from the both of you as I did our interviews and research!

Secondly, thank you to my husband Shane for your unwavering support during this process. I especially appreciate you checking in on me when I had been holed up in my office for a few hours writing, or bringing the cats by to say "hi." I am eternally grateful that you help me chase my dreams.

JASON

A heart-felt thank you to my wife, Cathy, for putting up with early morning and late-night writing sessions (and maybe even a few bitch sessions). You kept me going, even when I thought I wanted to stop writing. To my daughters, Megan, Bayley, Emily, and Shelly. You make me want to be better every day.

I also wish to thank my co-authors Chelsea and Sheila. This has been a wild journey and I am so happy to have experienced it with the two of you. Through all of our writing sessions and conversations, I have learned so much. You two are the epitome of great educators. Even when we experienced our own tensions while writing the book, you kept us focused. It is an honor and privilege to have co-authored this book with both of you. I look forward to future writing journeys with both of you.

The authors would like to thank the teachers and the administrators that shared their personal stories with us. They were our inspiration for the book. Thank you for your courage and dedication to your students and our profession. We would also like to thank Natalie Buhl and Dr. Amy LaPierre for their feedback on early drafts of the manuscript. Thank you to Ben Paplham for your help with the final manuscript. Thank you to Dr. Barbara Sramek, for taking the time to write the foreword. We are forever grateful. Finally, thank you to Tom Koerner and Kira Hall, our editing team at Rowman & Littlefield. Your support, feedback, and patience were appreciated. We could not have completed this book without you.

And to all those who find their way into education as administrators, teachers, aides, coaches, food service, maintenance, bus drivers, crossing guards, office staff: we salute you for your service to students. And to any educators who read this book and decide to use your vulnerabilities to lean into facing your tensions, we congratulate you on taking the first steps towards possibly lessening some of the tensions in your work lives.

Introduction

RESOLUTIONS

For many that first week of a brand-new year, resolutions are set, goals established, plans created, and motivation is there to follow through with all of them. The first week of the new year feels great! Many are ready to make a difference in the new year, creating their new self.

Resolutions include getting healthy / eating healthier / working out more. And during that first week, the refrigerator looks great: full of colorful fruits and vegetables already cut up due to motivated meal prepping. A gym bag has already been packed and repacked three days during that first week of preparation for getting to the gym and working out, moving their body, pushing themselves harder than other times because right now they are MOTIVATED! They want to feel great!

And then the weekend hits, or that last holiday party, or their overall motivation begins to wane. Maybe they have run out of their carefully planned food, and let's be serious—every single muscle in their body hurts, including muscles they didn't even realize they used during workouts and food prep. Maybe they acknowledge that maybe they did not stretch the way that they should have to continue to prepare for this new year's resolution, this new self.

The lack of stretching and body aching for every menial task, ritualistic things, tricks people into going back to their old eating habits, and suddenly they find that their enthusiasm to continue with the resolutions, goals, and plans wanes. That next moment, the time when old habits are calling back to people, while new habits are guilting them, that right there—that is TENSION!

This book is about these very moments in professional lives. Everyone has those moments when the things they enjoy and appreciate about their jobs get lost in the day-to-day realities. They forget to stretch, they jump right in, or their mind tries to convince them that the opposite action would be better in a situation. As much as they'd like it to, the tension does not just go away.

In these moments they often lose motivation because they are afraid of the painful aftereffects or their mind tells them nothing is going to change, so why do anything about the tension. Unless they've pulled something, sore muscles go away over time, but with tension, it only builds. As it builds it can be compounded by other events until that tension is ready to drive them mad.

Consider a tension band (going all-in on the exercise analogies here). The whole purpose of a tension band is to first stretch, then be pulled in various directions, depending on its use. If someone has a band around their legs while they are doing squats, they expand outward. If they are using them to do bicep curls, they stretch. A tension band is pulled to its very brink, and perhaps there is a moment when they worry that it will break and hit them in the face.

But the more they use the tension band, the more comfortable they become with it. Perhaps they are able to stretch it more each time they use it and the fear slowly starts to dissipate. Perhaps they look for bands with more tension to help them become stronger. By pulling on that tension band every day, they change, they grow, they feel stronger and more confident to move on to and conquer the next band.

It is not without challenges that individuals get to this point. It is not without doubt that gets them to that growth. The fear of the band breaking might not ever dissipate. There might be a point where the band has been stretched enough and it is no longer effective. There might be days the band goes untouched, or is completely avoided. There might be situations, people, or circumstances that force one to abandon the exercise early, giving up temporarily. There may be people who do not believe that working with a tension band is for them, because they are either well beyond the bands or they do not want to attempt the challenge.

The answer here is NO, there is *always* a reason to work that tension band. There is good that comes from it. Perhaps it is not the go-to exercise, but there is value in facing the daunting challenges that the band represents. These tension bands can always be adjusted, tightened, changed to fit the different needs in a particular moment. But the benefits one gets from doing a band workout are too beneficial to ignore.

Now, most likely when you picked up this book you had zero intention of talking fitness, or of connecting your own New Year's resolutions to a tension band workout. We want you to see that in order to make progress with whatever intentions you have in your life right now, facing your tensions strategically and with purpose can result in a newer you.

Tensions in our lives force us to think differently and, in some cases, act differently in order to deal with the struggles. The final result, however, can be a more confident *you* even after being stretched (sometimes too far) from the tension. Tensions in your life create that painful stretch, one that we oftentimes wish we could have avoided, one we hide from and sometimes do everything in our power to brush under the carpet. In doing the opposite, and instead attacking the tensions, we build muscle.

When we actually acknowledge the tensions in our lives that are impacting our progress, we can then begin working to find solutions to them. When we hide from the tensions, we get stuck in a rut of emotions and actions, leading to unpleasant situations wherever tension is present.

By picking up this book you are choosing growth. You are choosing to acknowledge the hard, the uncomfortable, sometimes downright painful things that are impacting your progress as a human. You are choosing to work through those moments to stretch yourself and to build the muscles necessary to grow and then ultimately attack new tensions. And we are here to guide you in this exercise. Welcome!

WHY TENSIONS?

Human nature is to avoid tense situations and the feelings they create. We might avoid a confrontation with a friend or colleague. We might try to ignore a task hanging over our head that we do not want to tackle for various reasons. To alleviate the stressful feelings caused by this tension we might take a yoga class or indulge in comfort foods or beverages. We may treat ourselves to a massage to feel more relaxed. Or we may try to ignore the tense situation, hoping it will go away, until the feelings build up internally and then we erupt into some emotion.

In these instances, we might never truly deal with the issues that are causing the tense feelings, this negative tension. Most often this happens when we feel that the stress and tension is ours alone—that we are the only ones experiencing it. We simply need to "deal with it." We are here to tell you that tension is real. That everyone experiences tensions and that you are not alone in your frustrations and the stress of those tensions.

The thing about tension, however, is that there will always be some tension. Whether it is a difficult situation in a work setting that needs to be dealt with, or the underlying need to always be the best educator you could be, there is always going to be some sort of tension in your life. The reality then becomes establishing practices for managing the tensions, and growing from them.

THE ELEPHANT IN THE ROOM

What would happen if, instead of ignoring tensions and hoping they will dissipate on their own, we faced the tensions head-on? If we gave name to them and stood up to them as we might a bully or a strong wind? What if we addressed the emotions, feelings, and negative thoughts linked to these tensions and took charge of them? Would that turn the stressors we face into positive ones and change how we view the tensions that impact us and make them positive tensions?

Tensions in an environment are the elephant in the room. They exist, they are everywhere. They are at the forefront of your mind in conversation with a colleague over a dispute regarding curriculum. They are hanging from the ceiling tiles when you enter the office of an administrator to discuss the support of a student. They are sitting there on the desk with you while you respond to a disgruntled parent.

And if tensions are everywhere, why not acknowledge their existence and then face them? Why cower from them or try to avoid the reality of their presence? Why not use acknowledgment, tools, and strategies for meeting that tension where it is at, digging at the root cause, and stretching our capacity to handle them? Why? Because it is hard. Just like stretching the tension band to its limits, we stretch ourselves to our limits when we wade into new emotional territory. But also like the tension band, if we keep working at it strategically and purposefully we can potentially alleviate the power that the tension has over us. We diminish its effect on the situation, invite it to the table, and then use its very existence to grow in our humanness. Rather than finding the elephant as a larger than life issue, we should reduce its ability to tower over us and feel that we have the control.

WHY NOW?

Our hope is that you can relate to the experiences of the stories that we share. You may possibly use this book to reflect upon instances of tension you have faced to understand your reaction. Or, you may use this book to look at tensions in your current situation and find ways to begin releasing the power they have over you. Tensions will always be present, but are there ways to face and manage them?

Introduction

In the field of education, tensions are consistently present. Meeting student needs, covering curricular material, communicating with stakeholders, physical and mental health conditions, and a pandemic are just a sampling of some of the tensions faced by administrators and teachers in academic settings.

We present this discussion about tensions as a guide you can use in this ever-changing educational world. In order to shape our discussion, we share the stories of twelve educators who were willing to share the tensions they face in their schools. We wanted to understand their life experiences as positioned in regard to the tensions that impact their lives.

WHAT TO EXPECT

We have developed this book as a tool that acknowledges the tensions experienced by teachers and educators in K–12 environments. This book will feature real stories that we hope will resonate with you, our reader, who might share similar tensions. However, even if a tension does not resonate with you, we believe you will still find information, tools, and strategies that will be helpful for a range of situations.

Both administrators and teachers will find this book useful. Administrators and community leaders will gain insight into practices that may be increasing tensions within their educational environments. Additionally, teachers may see ways in which administrators and education leaders act as buffers in potentially tension-filled situations. Tensions can be positive or negative, but most people associate them with anxiety and stress, so recognizing root causes will hopefully decrease these feelings.

This book will delve into some of the tensions experienced by our teachers and administrators. Interviews were conducted before the 2020–2021 pandemic, and educators' pre-pandemic stories will be correlated with research to help give a name to these tensions. Each chapter shares vignettes, research, tools, and strategies to deal with specific tensions shared by multiple educators. Finally, each chapter ends by asking you, our readers, to reflect on your own experiences and how they connected to the tension in order to move forward in your thinking about tensions.

Questions we hope to answer within the covers of this book include:

- How does one identify the root cause of tension in order to better deal with it?
- What if we address the emotions, feelings, and negative thoughts linked to the tensions in our lives and take charge of them? Would this act ultimately change how we view the tensions that impact us?
- Are there such things as positive tensions?

While writing this book, we made some assumptions about the districts, schools, administrators, and teachers that may or may not be addressed in this book:

- We assume that student needs are at the forefront of all that our teachers do. Therefore, our questions do not focus on students per se, but student social, emotional, and academic growth is embedded in responses.
- We assume all of our educators were effective. Each of them had been employed for multiple years so we assume their respective districts viewed each as a good administrator or teacher.
- We assume that all the educators were part of districts working to improve racial and gender equity in their schools. Tensions were not presented to participants by the interviewers. Instead, each educator described his or her own stressors and some of these were related to issues of equity.
- We assume the identity of "educators" as teachers, principals, superintendents, and any other stakeholders in a school system. When necessary, we assume the name "teachers" as those who have daily classroom responsibilities with students. When necessary, we assume the name "administrators" as principals and assistant principals. Other administrative titles are used when necessary, but will be defined by the scenario.
- We assume each story that was shared can be viewed through multiple lenses. Therefore, stories may reappear within book chapters but be analyzed through different perspectives.

Stick with us on this journey. It may be painful to come face-to-face with some of the tensions that you might be ignoring, but we hope it is actually more cathartic and freeing to give a name to them and deal with the root causes. Tension will always be with each of us, but we hope that you will be able to find ways to deal with some of the more pressing tensions that may be holding you back from reaching your goals, reaching your plans, and finding your motivation. Full disclosure: you may want to stretch your mind and body a bit first. Here we go.

REFLECTIVE QUESTIONS

1. What was your motivation for picking up this book?
2. What are some of your goals, and plans (also known as resolutions) for your personal growth while reading this book?
3. How will you know if you are achieving these goals as you move forward?

Chapter 1

Tensions in Schools

Tensions in any environment are not unusual. The Oxford Dictionary defines tension as *the state of being stretched tightly* or *strain on mental capacities or emotions*. This basic definition of tension does not begin to cover the extent to which tensions impact daily life. Tensions can present themselves in a variety of ways throughout the course of our lives. Table 1.1 provides an inexhaustive list of examples of tensions.

Among other feelings, stress is an inherent part of the academic world for those whose role it is to design and implement systems that help students grow. It is not hyperbole to say that teachers and administrators in K–12 settings face multitudes of stressors on a daily basis which impact their abilities to successfully do the jobs they are tasked with, to love their jobs, and ultimately their ability to have an impact on students' lives.

And what happens if these stressors pile up or are not dealt with? Tension. Tension is a strained state. Mental faculties are stretched thin. Physical symptoms could appear. What happens when the stress of a particular situation has led to tensions is unexplored in literature. How does one identify the root cause of tension in order to better deal with it? That's what this book hopes to uncover. First, however, let's define tension.

Table 1.1 Examples of Tension

Type of Tension	Source of Tension
Personal	Intrapersonal conflicts, such as guilt, expectations, or self-ideation.
Relational	These can be personal, such as marriage, or work, such as a supervisor-employee relationship.
Family	Expectation of others, expectations on self from others, tension associated with care of others.
Cultural	Ascribing to the stereotypes of a culture and the corresponding intentional or unintentional stressors connected to the stereotype.

DEFINITIONS OF TENSIONS

In order to proceed in a conversation about tensions, it is vital to identify a working definition of this concept. According to multiple definitions, tension is an inner unrest, a state of opposition, or the act of being stretched. This book uses a working definition of tensions as physical, mental, and emotional strain that result from persistent conflicts, situations, or environments.

Tensions are often the result of a challenge to personal beliefs and can be either out in the open or completely hidden from view. People often feel tension as a personal attack, something that is out to "get us" or sap us of our mental faculties and energy. But while the presence of tension can result in feelings of being stretched or strained, it can ultimately result in either a positive or negative change in a person's thinking or actions.

Quick and Nelson (1998) support the idea of workplace tension. They define tension as "mental and emotional worries during work" and job tension as "the amount of psychological discomfort experienced on the job" (p. 571). They recognize that educational workplace stress, along with the accompanying psychological demand, is due to lack of learning opportunities, as well as poor social-organizational aspects.

An article by Lehne and Koelsch (2015) defines tension as "affective states that

a. are associated with conflict, dissonance, instability, or uncertainty,
b. create a yearning for resolution,
c. concern events of potential emotional significance, and
d. build on future-directed processes of expectation, anticipation, and prediction." (p. 2)

This comprehensive definition recognizes that tension is multifaceted, personal, and can have long-term effects. The yearning for a resolution recognizes that tension produces a state of discomfort, one that individuals experiencing tension wish to end, or go away. Oftentimes with tension people prefer to move on or forget about it rather than deal with an uncomfortable situation. Another option is to meet the tension head-on and create a solution from the tense experience.

Part of the definition, however, says that even though one moves on from the experience, or finds resolutions, there are lasting effects.

The final aspect of the definition discusses the growth that can come from the tension. Lehne and Koelsch's article states: "Assuming that uncertainty is resolved after the first exposure, subsequent exposures should have lost their power to create tension" (p. 5); repeated experiences of the initial tension can diminish the response the tension elicits if the tension is appropriately dealt with the first time.

If the tension is "swept under the rug" then the personal growth of dealing with the tension has not occurred, and therefore cannot be used to lessen the tension the next time it arises. Tensions themselves do not cause growth, but when tension is addressed in a positive manner, it can possibly be beneficial for the person who is experiencing the tension-filled situation.

While this sounds incredibly productive when dealing with tensions, the article does go on to acknowledge that "in some contexts, tension experiences seem to be resistant against the loss of uncertainty associated with repeated exposures" (p. 5). This is oftentimes associated with the depth of emotional responses associated with the first experience. Meaning, an experience that creates deep stress or fear from the tension will not be as easy to simply resolve through repeated exposures. The new emotion, namely fear, takes precedence over the personal growth and hinders the ability to quell the tension.

Lehne and Koelsch (2015) recognize that for many, the definition of tension has mostly all negative connotations associated with it. The researchers do not believe that tensions need to be only negative. They state:

> In some contexts, experiences of tension are associated with negative emotions such as fear, concern, or distress, which are generally tried to be avoided; in other contexts, tension is experienced as positive, and can, in fact, be a major motivator to engage in certain activities. The appeal of many forms of media entertainment such as music, film, or literature, for example, often seems to directly derive from their power to evoke feelings of tension and suspense. Similarly, tension is experienced in a multitude of everyday life situations, most typically during the anticipation of uncertain but (potentially) significant events (e.g., medical diagnoses, exams, job interviews, etc.). (p. 1)

Positive tensions can be as motivating as negative ones. With negative tensions, individuals work to avoid or disassociate themselves from the experience. They use these situations as motivators to reduce tension in their lives. With positive tensions, however, they are motivated to grow, experience the emotions, and challenge themselves because of the tension. Instead of avoidance, they embrace the experience for the growth potential that it has.

Tensions in any environment are not unusual. However, the K–12 education setting is one in which there are numerous tensions that could not only have an effect on how a school environment operates but also impact student achievement and growth. Therefore, the tensions within a school are multiplied as impacted groups with individuals experiencing tension join other groups and take on their tensions. These groups are an important component when trying to understand tensions, as each has its own strains or ways of being stretched.

A 2018 OECD survey called the Teaching and Learning International Survey (TALIS) found that in the forty-eight countries that took part in the survey, 26 percent of teachers felt like their work is valued by their societies. Approximately 18 percent of these teachers said they experienced a lot of stress in their work (OECD, 2020), but the report noted that this stress could have cultural connections depending upon the economy and needs of the countries surveyed.

Thirty percent of teachers reported experiencing stress "a lot" in England, whereas only 5 percent of teachers in the Russian Federation responded "a lot" to the same query. Female teachers tended to experience more stress than males, teachers under thirty experienced more stress than teachers age fifty or above, and those working in schools in city areas experienced more stress than those in villages or rural areas.

Specific areas of stress were broken into three categories: workload, student behavior, and responsiveness to stakeholders (OECD, 2020). The top four expectations cited that caused teachers "a lot" or "quite a bit" of stress included having too much administrative work to do, being responsible for students' achievements, having too much work, and keeping up with changing requirements (OECD, 2020, p. 95).

In the same OECD study, administrators cited specific instances that created stress. Having too much administrative work along with keeping up with changing requirements, being held responsible for students' achievements, and addressing parent or guardian concerns were listed as some of their higher sources of stress (OECD, 2020, p. 95). These are challenges that administrators could have perhaps anticipated when taking on their leadership roles, yet they still create tension.

Understanding the specific underlying expectations and how they are interpreted, followed, and reflected upon by both teachers and administrators may help to uncover patterns and create a pathway to dealing with tensions. It is not too far off to assume that the following sources of tension are similar in school systems across the United States.

Groups in a school system that can both cause tension and be impacted by tension include: district level administrators and principals, teachers, students, staff, parents, and other stakeholders who have a role in the ventures of a particular school. The number of individuals in these groups increases the areas in which tension can arise. Tensions can fester and grow both within and among these groups depending upon the tasks that the members need to complete. The goal was to determine some of the major tensions and what can be done about them.

THE PROCESS

In order to understand some of the tensions experienced by K–12 educators, a group of teachers and administrators volunteered to share their experiences. These discussions, in which their stories were collected via personal interviews and then analyzed for consistent themes regarding tensions, asked educators about both perceived positive and negative tensions they experience in their respective roles. The teachers and administrators who volunteered represented a wide variety in terms of years of experience, gender, subjects, and grade levels taught.

They also represented different educational environments; some participants worked in smaller districts with decreased levels of leadership and power within a district while others were part of larger districts where leadership and power could be very segmented. The leadership styles of administrators in these environments impacted the relationship between teachers and administrators, and determined whether there were open lines of communication between the two groups. Table 1.2 shows the pseudonym, role, and school setting of each person interviewed.

All subjects who were a part of the discussion were employees of public schools that generally had the same structure within their respective districts: administrators presided over district decisions, building principals managed their schools, and within the schools were teams whose members were dependent on things such as grade level, subject taught, or content area. In the team structures, there was usually a designated person to be the group's representative, and then there were informal leaders who took on tasks above and beyond their own teaching duties out of a sense of duty to students or obligation to the team.

Subjects who took part in this multistep process volunteered of their own accord, expressing interest in sharing their tensions. They completed an initial survey in which they indicated whether they wanted to take part in this

Table 1.2 Pseudonyms for the Educators Who Were Interviewed

Teachers	Administrators
Nicole: High School	Matt: Elementary Principal
Ariel: Middle School	Antony: Elementary Principal
JoAnne: Elementary School	Leo: Elementary School Associate Principal
Macy: Elementary School	Mitch: High School Principal
Paula: Middle School	
Jeff: Middle/High School	
Craig: High School	
Delilah: Middle School	

book; they signed a permission form that would allow their stories to be told in this book; and they consented to an in-person interview or an online video interview, with the date and time to be chosen by them. At any time they had the option to back out of the process and their information would have been disregarded; none of the subjects chose this option.

THE THEMES

Whether a teacher or administrator, all were asked the same questions, with some wording changed for context, over the course of a forty-five-minute interview. The interviews were then transcribed and analyzed for consistent themes surrounding tension, as well as coping mechanisms that may have helped to soothe any negative tensions. During the analysis, it became very apparent that—even though these subjects volunteered, came from different education settings, and taught a variety of classes or led a variety of student populations—there are similar tensions that connect all of them.

After closely examining these tensions, they were then grouped with similar tensions and our main themes emerged. We found the positive and negative tensions they described fell into one of seven main themes:

- The System
- Colleagues
- Workload
- Students
- Parents
- Expectations
- Communication

What follows is a brief description of each of these themes based on the experiences of the educators. These descriptions are an overview, and the themes will be revisited throughout the chapters as they led to various conclusions and solutions.

Along with the discussion of themes presented here, an introduction of the participants is also included. The names here are pseudonyms to protect their privacy, but the vignettes represent the values and opinions of the participants. A general description is provided in order to set the context for the conversations held regarding tensions and the workplaces that the participants come from.

VIGNETTES AND THEME ANALYSIS

In this section we'll weave the stories of educators who took part in this interview while also exploring the themes these narratives uncovered.

Theme One: The System

Antony has been the principal of his suburban elementary school district for over twenty years. He held various administrative roles before settling in as a principal. Antony had never anticipated that he would become an administrator in his career—it just kind of happened during his college years. He has also been in charge of other initiatives in his district that help students with varying needs be successful academically.

The biggest source of tension for Antony is his inability to always do what is in the best interest of his building, teachers, and students because of mandates imposed upon education. Whether they are set by the federal government, state government, or the district, Antony feels that navigating those systems and trying to determine where the necessary boundaries are is a challenge. He looks to find which mandates make sense for his students, which are common sense, and what is the best way to provide services for his students. He feels the tensions when he has to manage rules and regulations with his staff that he himself may not personally support.

Antony views teachers as if they are his students. He feels the need to make sure they are taken care of, push them professionally without offending anyone, and has tough conversations when needed. The tension for him is to personally get over the desire to be liked when confronting an issue. Additionally, Antony understands the pressure of feeling like he has to have an answer to an issue right away. However, he believes he has learned in his career that it is okay to say, "I don't have that answer."

Antony enjoys his job and interacting with stakeholders in students' lives. However, it is sometimes the systems in education that hinder his ability to enjoy this, especially when he has to enforce the mandates that do not align with his beliefs. It is in these moments that his desire to have people like him is tested. While he wants to avoid people being mad at him he also has a duty to enforce the mandates.

Systemic tensions result from an organization's norms, in this case the educational structures put in place by the leaders of the group, whether it be superintendent, principal, or teacher leaders. In many educational environments, systemic norms can be broken down further in the *known* versus the *unknown* norms. Known norms are the ones that are explicitly stated or proposed: schedules, lesson plans, those things that are communicated to the people impacted by them.

Unknown norms are those that are implicit or unstated. These can include, but are not limited to, deciding on an appropriate time to talk to an administrator about an issue, where the line between being colleagues and friends is, and how to talk to a distraught parent. These unknown norms underlie many of the negative tensions felt by educators because they are not regulated and, therefore, people are nervous when trying to decipher what to do about them. Both known and unknown norms impact the culture of a district or school building.

The difference in the systemic norms lie within the expectations and communication between and among stakeholders. In most cases, the administrators of the settings were viewed to be the leaders and communicators of the educational environments. In most cases, a trusting and safe environment was seen as important to the members of an educational system, particularly when dealing with difficult issues.

The administrator, district or building, was key to the creation of the trusting and safe environment. Educational systems with a culture that was not built on trust or safety to openly communicate led to power struggles between administrators and teachers. The ensuing power struggles between administrators and teachers resulted in negative tensions throughout the school. The tension impacted teachers' levels of comfort within that school and ultimately their ability to do their jobs.

Other norms of a system that impact the amount of negative tension felt by teachers and administrators included the capacity to have tough conversations when needed. Making people unhappy and ruining friendships were seen as barriers to having tough conversations. An additional cause of negative tensions is how discipline—the discipline of both students and adults—were or were not addressed by administrators. When a clear-cut method to address discipline situations was in place, negative tensions were reduced. When a vague method of discipline was in place, the tension tended to be higher.

Matt is currently an administrator at a large K–6 school. His career hasn't always been in administration; he began his educational career in middle level education. Matt came to his current district as an assistant principal in a middle school, then took on the role of elementary principal and early childhood coordinator, before moving to his current role as principal at the second-largest school in his district.

In this role, Matt relies on the systems that are in place to guide his actions. He spoke about the need to understand both the district and administrators' roles in the system. The administrators he works with form a tight-knit group.

With his teachers, Matt created a system that involves him shouldering most of the difficult decisions and then communicating those with staff.

Matt credits the relationship that he has built with his administrator colleagues as being the most successful endeavor in his current role and pointed to their efforts to be consistent in messaging and actions throughout the district. "What we have really focused on the last three years is we really want consistency among all elementaries." While for many, the systemic control of educational environments creates tension, Matt recognizes that the individuals at the district level, in roles similar to his, help deflate these tensions with the use of structural policies put in place.

Matt does experience tension in his day-to-day interactions with staff, students, and families. However, he relies on the district's system and that of his building to help guide his actions through those experiences. When a mandate is put in place by the district, a sense of unity helps enforce any actions associated with it. Messaging is important to Matt and his colleagues.

Matt gave the example of a teacher who continued to teach a topic that had been removed by the district, referring to the number of times he has had to be in communication with this teacher. It was a source of tension, but Matt's plan of action was supported by requirements at the district level. Because of the systems in place, Matt could continue to focus on the relationships with his staff and colleagues because the roles and duties were clearly laid out and did not need to be invented.

Theme Two: Colleagues

Colleagues are people who work closely together. They are members of a team. For many educators, colleagues can include both peers and supervisors within the school system. Colleagues could be part of an immediate team, or they may be part of the larger school environment. To teachers, this could mean that they teach the same subject, grade, or provide support within a class.

To administrators, this could be other administrators within or outside of their schools, but also could mean the individuals they interact most with on a daily basis, such as their administrative support teams. While some of the participants would group their administrators in as colleagues, most interviewees defined colleagues as individuals at the same power level who tended to share the same type of responsibilities as them.

One tension vocalized numerous times was communication. This seemed to be a predominant theme especially when tension already existed between colleagues. Colleagues felt tension just in broaching the subject at the center of a conflict; they also felt tension in discussing issues. This was an especially prominent concern among administrators who were conscious of their conversations with teachers and how the conversations would impact the overall climate on that team in the school.

Administrators discussed being cognizant about what could happen to the working relationship once a difficult conversation is initiated. This was a recurring negative tension that administrators felt. While they acknowledged the tension the impending conversation created, they also recognized the need for difficult, honest conversations with teachers to sometimes aid in the climate at school.

Tensions between colleagues were not always negative in scope as some resulted in positive outcomes. First, it was possible for a team to become stronger when common issues were faced. This was true for teacher-to-teacher relationships as well as administrator-to-teacher relationships. A participant felt slighted by her administrator's Professional Learning Community (PLC) leadership. The pair had a candid conversation regarding the issue, which allowed her to air her grievance and understand the intentions of the administrator. The result was that the relationship greatly improved due to the conversation.

A second positive effect that emerged from tensions among colleagues was a greater understanding of a colleague's perspective. It was qualified that this was most successful when the effort was put forth to understand the experiences, philosophy, and fears of a co-worker with whom one dissents. This willingness to be open to their colleague's understanding based on their experiences allowed for a deeper understanding of their colleague and why that opinion would be held so strongly. It also allowed for better communication in the future, understanding where each other was coming from.

While colleagues can be a source of tension, they were also found to be an important resource for alleviating tensions. This held true when a teacher or administrator considered a co-worker or group of co-workers as a safe space to explore issues surrounding a particular tension. Participants referred to having a "tribe," a "team," or someone "I could go to" at school when they were feeling stressed or overwhelmed by tension. These relationships were represented in examples across teacher-to-teacher, administrator-to-administrator, and, in one case, teacher-to-administrator.

It is important to note that there were mixed messages about the relationship between teacher and administrator. Some teachers felt more comfortable going to their administrator than another teacher with concerns, while other teachers felt going to their administrator would cause a strain on the relationship. Administrators tended to rely on other administrators for collegiality, while some had a small number of teachers they considered to be members of their close group. Overall, relationships with those around the teachers and administrators in an educational environment were both a cause of tension as well as a resource for relief when dealt with.

JoAnne is an elementary classroom teacher in a suburban district who has great pride in the teaching profession. She feels her district provides teachers with a lot of resources and professional development. She has confidence in her skills as a teacher and communicator, but gets frustrated when colleagues have the potential to improve or enhance their teaching practice for the sake of students but don't. This is her biggest source of tension—how to get teachers to realize they have the power. "That tension comes with the unknown and being embarrassed by what we didn't know, and needing to learn it. There's a lot of discomfort around that."

JoAnne has a strong relationship with her principal and cites this, and her improved relationships with colleagues, as a means to decrease the tension. JoAnne has high expectations of herself and others, and is continually searching for ways to help those around her become stronger teachers for their students. She has pursued higher education in fields that will allow her to train teachers to be advocates for students.

She feels passionately that all students can learn and is on committees and district initiatives that address equity. She mentioned that racial tensions are one of the areas she would like to focus on, helping colleagues understand biases and perspectives. Additionally, JoAnne is a strong advocate for students receiving special education services, believing that students in these programs deserve rigor and high expectations.

JoAnne has an interest in teacher leadership. She admits that she does not like it when someone, such as a curriculum coach, is put on her team because she senses that they do not appreciate or understand the work she is already doing to help her students. JoAnne recounted times when situations like these were stressful for her, but she had to step back and look at the perspective of the coach. When she is under tension, JoAnne tends to talk it out with people on the other side of the stress and then she tries to see the situation from that person's point of view. Discussing troubling situations with people was a strength of JoAnne's.

Theme Three: Workload

Ariel is in her twenty-third year as a middle school teacher. She loves working with students and giving them opportunities to be creative. Over the years, she has taken on leadership in a variety of roles, some student-based and others teacher-oriented. Her passion is in sharing information effectively so that everyone can do the jobs to the best of their abilities. Her tension is that she sometimes takes on too many roles.

Ariel has had to find ways to manage her workload as teacher, leader, group advisor, and committee member as they often overlap in their timelines. Ultimately, she is a teacher, but her time is split into many different factions.

Ariel acknowledges that this is her choice and that over time she has had to learn to do things immediately or they tend not to get done. Procrastination is not an option in her daily routine.

Oddly, however, it is not the workload that causes Ariel the most amount of stress. It is any changes to the routine that cause her tension. Because she has only so much time to devote to her roles, anything different in a day's plan can cause her stress. Whether it's because her time management is off, or because student behavior changes with an altered schedule, Ariel wishes that student behavior could be taken into consideration when changes to schedules are made.

Ariel has acclimated to some of the usual stressors of teaching. She has worked with a number of colleagues in her years, so she has adapted to changes. She sees parents as protecting their children, so when they call or email with questions she does not take things personally. Student behaviors can be a source of stress, but Ariel tries to deal with these types of situations within her classroom.

With a lot of the stressors in education, Ariel has to continually manage her workload so that she is not overwhelmed. She would not recommend that other teachers, particularly new teachers, take on so many roles, but she feels that through them she has grown as a teacher and a leader. Without the support of her administration she does not feel that she would be the teacher she is.

Workload tension is best described as the overall demands of working in a K–12 setting. Typically, most tensions come from external sources. Examples of these tensions include, but are not limited to the day-to-day interactions with students, interpersonal relations, classroom management, lesson planning and execution of lessons, understanding student needs, differentiation, and grading and reporting grades. It also includes tensions that relate to communication with a variety of parties, such as responding to emails and phone calls to parents, administrators, and team members.

There are also extra duties and completing professional duties such as work with curriculum, evaluations of teachers, and completing paperwork and referrals as they relate to the students in the class. One of the largest areas of negative tensions from workload was the result of not having control over a variety of variables and not knowing what issues lie ahead as relates to classroom practices.

Additionally, lack of time to deal with the tensions was cited as a negative in regard to completing all of the workload duties. Teachers' days are regimented, and administrators have a rotating series of issues to deal with on any given day. There was a mix between those who took the workload home to deal with it outside of the school day, versus those who consciously tried to leave the work at school so they could focus on their own families and personal needs.

Three solutions were uncovered to help alleviate tensions associated with workload. The first is finding ways to physically handle the tension so students are never aware of rising tensions. These might include breathing techniques, physical activity, or talking with colleagues. All educators interviewed were adamant that they did not want students to sense any negative tension. Secondly, when a district is well resourced in terms of materials and personnel, this helps alleviate negative tensions because teachers and administrators feel they have the tools necessary to combat the tensions as they arise.

And finally, quality professional development was cited as a positive way to work through negative tensions associated with workload. Staff meetings, team meetings, professional development days with a focus, professional learning communities (PLCs), and graduate and doctoral work were cited as ways to relieve tension. However, meetings and professional development that are not focused or goal-oriented were seen as adding to the negative tensions.

Paula is currently a veteran teacher at a suburban school and has held many roles as both a curricular area teacher and a teacher of non-core subjects (e.g., art, music, physical education) classes—the non-core subject is the position she currently holds. Paula has been with the same district for the duration of her twenty-plus years in teaching. Paula's teaching philosophy is student-centered, one in which she strives to make each situation a win-win for every individual.

Paula works to provide authentic learning opportunities for her students by bringing in volunteers, teaching life lessons as they arise, and modeling appropriate responses to situations. Being able to adjust on the fly is a skill that Paula feels she utilizes well in her crowded classroom environment with more students than her classroom was designed to accommodate. While she would like to see a few things changed, overall she feels she uses her resources well.

While she encounters challenges with differentiation, student needs, and class size, Paula's tensions involve her workload expectations. These include daily tasks such as checking emails, taking attendance, responding to parent concerns, and planning her program. The biggest expectation that is a source of tension for Paula is the evaluation of teachers. The process her school, district, and state utilizes does not fit with Paula's teaching style. She feels there is a lot of paperwork that adds stress to a teacher's workload.

Paula would rather have observations and evaluations of her work to be as authentic as possible, preferably where an administrator comes in her room to observe and take notes with a conversation taking place afterward. The time that is utilized trying to meet the expectations is a tension, but Paula focuses on her students. "Each day I try to say this is a blank slate, okay, gonna try to forget what happened yesterday. Today we're going to start all over again."

Theme Four: Students

For the most part, those interviewed did not mention feelings of negative tension with students themselves. In fact, it was the opposite. The recurring theme from teachers and administrators was they loved their jobs and loved working with the students; the term *passion* was used frequently in this regard. Negative tensions with students arose when there was a need to discipline a student and a disagreement occurred when there was a discrepancy between what teachers wanted to do versus what they had to do according to administrative policy.

Tensions with students often revolved around how an administrator viewed or handled discipline versus how a teacher thought the situation should be resolved. Some teachers felt administrators need strict guidelines and should follow them; when a discipline issue reached an administrator there were differences between the idea of applying leniency or adhering to the school's discipline policy.

An example cited for this was when a teacher needed to send a student to the office due to a behavioral issue. The principal returned by asking the teacher to be in touch with the parent to report that the student has had some issues. The teacher recalled having taken that step already and felt frustrated, feeling the disciplining fell to them when they had already tried everything and were seeking the help and support of the administrator. This created a negative tension for that teacher.

The main source of tension for both teachers and administrators lies in helping students achieve academic growth while understanding and using best practices in an effective manner. Teachers found that tension arose when a curricular series moved on in a unit of study, such as mathematics, where some students may not have mastered the current content that they would need to understand within the next unit. The teacher felt administration did not understand the issue and thus became conflicted about the ambiguity to move forward in the content or not to move on.

Finally, when it comes to their students' best interests, roles of support staff and supportive educational services could create tensions for teachers. Teachers generally did not understand the role of special education services and how to best work in tandem with those services in order to do what is best for the student. Teachers often expressed confusion about making modifications based on individual education plans, particularly when the overall goals for the student as guided by special education services did not match with the teacher's philosophies.

For example, one teacher cited how a special education teacher's goal for a particular student did not match the expectation that the teacher had for the student. This expectation was not specified through the student's IEP (Individualized Education Plan); therefore, that document provided little to clarify expectations. Tensions arose when the two educational professionals did not agree on how best to assist that student, which speaks to this section's theme on the challenge to create rigorous academic goals for students based on individual data, develop a coherent plan, and implement that plan for the student's best interest.

Craig, a teacher in his last year before retirement, was excited to talk about tension in the K–12 setting. After holding a variety of roles including teacher and effectiveness coach in the same district within a large, urban setting, Craig had returned to the classroom to finish his teaching career helping students recover credits. Craig is most proud of his ability to connect with students. "If you hear a kid complain they say 'you never listen to me,' which is number one, so I just make sure that I listen."

Craig enjoyed working with students his first year back in the classroom, but his administrator was not helpful and actually suggested things that made Craig uncomfortable about the work he would be doing. This strife continued for an entire school year and Craig began to question his worth and his ability to work with students. His self-esteem plummeted as he was unsure if he should continue the work he had started.

Craig decided to stick with the position. The next school year began with a new administrator who understood Craig's philosophy of "students first," and worked with him to create a viable and successful program. Craig was also able to find a group of people with which to collaborate, and he feels that he has again found his self-efficacy in working with student and confidence in his teaching abilities.

Theme Five: Parents

Teachers and administrators said that tension with parents was often sporadic; neither felt ongoing tension. Most often, negative tensions appeared when a miscommunication occurred between school and home, or when there was an unresolved or unknown issue hanging over those involved. An example of miscommunication could begin with a student lying to parents and guardians about a school situation, or school policy infractions.

In both types of instances the point of miscommunication occurred because parents disagreed with the way these situations were handled. As a result, parents tended to contact school personnel to discuss the matter, typically when they were upset, which added negative tension to an already intense situation. Teachers mentioned the fact that they sometimes felt tension when first confronted by parents.

Negative tensions were also in abundance as numerous teachers and administrators discussed the stress that occurs when they receive an angry, unexpected voice message or email from a parent. One teacher mentioned the fear associated with the idea of being "ambushed" by a parent, particularly if there are a series of issues that parents feel need to be addressed immediately.

Neither teachers nor administrators enjoyed the unknown issues that lie in wait, particularly when they felt they were being attacked. However, when an issue was resolved and all parties were satisfied, a positive feeling usually replaced the negativity brought on by the initial tension. Very little was mentioned about the dynamic of a teacher initiating the communication with a parent and tensions that might go along with that scenario.

Macy has spent her eight-year teaching career situated at the same elementary school in the primary ages. Her district neighbors a metropolitan area, but is a suburban district to that area. During that time, she has had the opportunity to further her own education by both completing a master's degree in school leadership as well as obtaining a reading specialist license. Macy has been fortunate enough to have worked with two different administrators and feels that her administrators often filter tensions regarding the "unknown" for her and fellow staff members and appreciates this particularly when there is a tense situation.

Macy feels she has a good relationship with many of her students' parents, but there are times when these relationships can be stressful. Macy enjoys interacting with the parents of her students, but she finds the most tension arises when she views a parent as attacking her for some situation. In these instances, Macy feels the tension personally and tries to find ways to dissipate the emotions. She might talk to colleagues. She might exercise. She strives to be the best teacher that she can be, but instances where she feels a conflict with a parent do cause her to reflect upon whether she is doing the right thing.

Macy enjoys teaching and works to implement best practices in her daily lessons. Macy also expects her colleagues to do their best for students in their own classrooms. When she doesn't feel this is happening, Macy gets frustrated. She wants to talk to her administrator about some of the things that are causing tension, but she is unsure of what her role is in the school system. Would her principal appreciate the information? Would her colleagues be upset?

Macy enjoys spending time with her colleagues outside of school. She sees the value in colleagues having a relationship outside of school. So, when there is a conflict in school, Macy tends not to deal with it forcefully because she doesn't want to offend her friends. This is a conundrum for Macy because she does not know how to handle the situation in a way that resolves the problems but manages to maintain relationships.

Theme Six: Expectations

Both internal and external expectations were noted as sources of tension by teachers and administrators. Internal tensions were described as those that a teacher or administrator places on themself. These internal tensions can be positive or negative in nature. They were seen as positive if they helped the educator grow in some way: personally, intellectually, emotionally, or philosophically.

However, internal expectations elicited some of the strongest language in terms of how teachers and administrators felt. These educators questioned if they were doing their best for students, were always striving to improve, did not want to feel incompetent, or were constantly rethinking decisions. These internal struggles often filtered to issues with colleagues when colleagues were held to these same internal standards held by those interviewed.

External expectations were those placed on teachers and administrators by outside sources; these were cited in the workload section above. However, an external tension that arose numerous times included curriculum issues that did not align with an educator's teaching philosophy. Educators wondered how to remain true to their core beliefs when they had to promote or follow a program that belied their pedagogy.

These were generally cited as negative tensions, although some teachers saw them as opportunities for growth, especially in instances where the adopted model went against their personal philosophical beliefs. Administrators' curricular tensions were negative when the administrator was not familiar with a content area or a specific program that was being used. They wondered how to get teachers on board with the program when they themselves did not necessarily see the entire value. In these instances, administrators referenced being knowledgeable in a variety of areas to help in their decision-making as leaders.

Interestingly, there were exceptions to tensions associated with curriculum. Instances where teachers and administrators were allowed some flexibility to differentiate based on student needs generally created more positive feelings about curriculum. There was one particular curricular program that a teacher mentioned absolutely hating because that school was being held to the rigid pacing of the content, but another teacher absolutely loved the exact same program because that school was allowed to alter the lessons based on student progress.

With all the internal and external expectations, it became apparent that the struggle for many educators here is the level of expectations they place on themselves in regard to planning and implementing effective lessons, growing student achievement, managing student behavior, communicating with parents, and working efficiently with colleagues. For many, their own school experiences were positive. They were successful. They completed their assignments. They had high personal expectations. And thus, the majority of the teachers indicated they are internally motivated.

This leads to issues of self-efficacy, the belief a teacher has in the ability to do their job, when intrinsic motivation is tied to the success of external variables. For example, teachers who have students who misbehave or do not follow class rules when there is a substitute teacher for a day tended to take that misbehavior personally, wondering what they could have done to prepare the students more or to help the guest teacher. Even though they were not there, they indicated the behavior was tied to their self-worth as an effective teacher.

When students did not do well on an assessment, teachers tended to take this personally. When a teacher or teaching aide worked with a student in a manner that is not deemed as best practice by the classroom teacher, that classroom teacher took it personally, and many teachers tried to change the offending practice, even though it might not have been their student or their aide or even their content area. Many teachers took on these issues as their own and struggled with how to manage them, adding their perceived expectations of others to their already full plates.

Jeff is a teacher with over ten years experience in both high school and middle school. He teaches in a small district where the organization has the feel of a family. Jeff appreciates his administration's efforts to communicate with staff and feels that he can go to them with any questions or concerns he might have. Jeff is a bit more hesitant to talk with colleagues regarding issues and attributes this to his easy-going personality; he doesn't like to operate in a tense environment.

Jeff generally views tensions as opportunities for growth, even enjoying the process of things such as curriculum analysis. For example, where some might see new initiatives imposed by a district as an annoyance or hindrance, Jeff thinks of them as opportunities to look at current practices in order to decide which should stay and which need to be enhanced or changed. He prefers to look at these types of things through a positive lens.

The biggest source of tension for Jeff is understanding modifications made for the special education students in his class. As a teacher, he has a set of expectations for himself and his students, but feels that when special education students are pulled from his class to take tests or work on assignments, they receive a level of assistance that is not in line with his expectations. Jeff does not feel comfortable asking the special education teachers or aides about this, as he does not want to impact their relationship in this family-like setting, so he has instead indicated to his administrators his concerns, to no avail.

Jeff feels he has a good relationship with students. He tends to deal with discipline problems in his classroom, as he is not always in agreement with how his district handles student discipline. To that end, Jeff feels he has a good relationship with the parents of his students; most often when tensions arise it is because of an untrue story that a student shared at home that upset the parents. When Jeff sees he has a voicemail, he gets nervous, but he is usually able to resolve the situations he's faced.

Theme Seven: Communication

Delilah is a teacher in her twelfth year as an educator. She has split that time between elementary and middle school teaching. She has worked for multiple administrators and finds it fascinating to see how workplaces evolve and change when the leadership styles of those at the top are different. Her biggest source of tension is the feeling of being in a power struggle with someone, and she continually looks for ways to avoid these.

Delilah constantly thinks about the teaching decisions she makes and even how to ask for permission to do something when needed, because she does not want to annoy anyone, particularly administrators. She is worried about the stress or tension any miscommunication might cause. There are topics she avoids to preserve this peace, which is important to keep her tension levels down.

Delilah is a self-professed people-pleaser and, at times, finds herself doing things she may not naturally do because she wants someone to be happy with her performance. She will overdo her performance when being observed by administrators. She might even do extra work for a professor to gain approval, or she might ignore a situation because she is afraid of the power struggle.

Yet when Delilah feels passionately regarding a topic she is knowledgeable about, she has no concerns with bringing this to the attention of whoever is making the decisions. For example, she has completed research on best practices for student performance and was not hesitant to approach all levels of administration with information about how a current program was impacting students and teachers.

Delilah's experiences with administrators have shaped her perspective. While she feels supported when it comes to issues with students or parents, one of her biggest sources of tension arose when an administrator did not put her in a teacher leader role that Delilah felt she was already doing. This source of stress was still very much a part of Delilah's thinking, and she cited this as a reason for making a big change in her career.

Delilah admits her own reaction, as well as the lack of communication on the administrator's part, were reasons for this escalation in stress. Delilah was already doing many of the duties, so she felt slighted that she was not given the role officially. She admits that she did not handle the situation well, but feels it would have helped if her administrator would have explained the reasons why she did not acquire the position. In this case, lack of communication had a detrimental effect on Delilah's ability and desire to do her job.

Delilah has a passion for helping students reach their potential. She often implements movement and critical thinking exercises into her lessons. She gives students choice and voice in assignments. It is very apparent that students' motivation is an important facet of Delilah's teaching practice. Her use of unique strategies demonstrates a desire to look for strategies to engage students in a variety of ways.

Mitch is an administrator in his fourteenth year in education, and has seen his responsibilities grow at each new step of his career trajectory into administration. Mitch began his educational career as a high school teacher in a suburban district and later took on a role in an administrative position at that school. Mitch left this district to accept the role of an assistant principal at an urban school district, and then became principal in another district.

As an administrator, Mitch works most closely with discipline, student services, and families. Mitch finds his strengths to be his diversity of thought and his leadership abilities. Mitch promotes text studies to help his staff understand philosophies that he holds important, showing that these philosophies are research driven and supported in a wider community.

Mitch believes that tensions are created due to three main things: clarity and communication, mission and vision misalignments, and leadership philosophies. He believes that tensions can be positive or negative depending on the impact on student success. Mitch believes that "any teacher who wants to be part of the (committee or decision-making) process should have the opportunity to do so," encouraging his teachers to be leaders in their school. Although Mitch fights the battle of his age and experience on a regular basis, he is willing to engage in conversations that lead to resolutions that impact his school, staff, and students.

Communication was an overarching tension, negative when it was not done to the participants' expectations and positive when educators felt like they had enough information to move forward. While communication is interwoven through a variety of the aforementioned subtopics and varies in style, its presence warranted its own category. While the questions were careful to not explicitly name communication in any of the prompting questions, it still was an area that emerged as a source of tension for each participant that was interviewed.

Tensions connected to communication arose due to the amount of contact needed, the lack of time for efficient delivery, desired outcomes, and direct versus indirect messaging. Relationally, communication was a tension in each level of interaction between teachers and students, teachers and families or community, teacher to teacher, and teacher to administration. Administrators also expressed these areas of communication as sources of tensions.

Tension due to communication was one that many of the participants could readily come up with concrete examples to share. This includes examples of administrators having a tension-filled conversation with a teacher regarding outdated teaching practices. It also included teachers communicating with administration regarding the increase of class sizes that literally no longer fit in their classroom, and the needs of those increased numbers.

Another example cited was between teacher and teacher, and the desire by one of the teachers to speak to a colleague about contributions to the larger grade level team but either not being ready to or not having the social skills necessary to approach the colleague. No matter the memory, each of our participants was quick to cite moments of tension that surrounded a "big" conversation they needed to have, and the tensions that led up to those conversations.

While an actual conversation brought tension, a lack of conversation brought just as much tension. Participants also cited the fact that not having a conversation was also a great source of tension. This included moments they felt they should have been kept in the loop, or should have been brought into the loop due to their expertise. It also included moments where they felt that administration should be stepping into the conversation but was not.

Leo has been in education for the past eleven years and has had the opportunity to hold multiple educational support roles during that time. Leo began his career as a support teacher to special education. During this time, he also completed his master's degree in school counseling. Leo secured a job as a school counselor at a middle school in a suburban school district. He earned a degree in school leadership, which allowed him to move into the role of Dean of Students at that middle school. After being in that role for a year, Leo moved on to be an associate principal at an elementary school and just finished his second year.

Leo knows that he is not a curriculum specialist, so he relies on the expert teachers in his building to help him learn the process. This is a source of tension for him; he stated that teachers may not be willing to have his help because he has never been a classroom teacher. He believes that this might be one of his biggest weaknesses, so he uses his time to learn about curricular standards, how many minutes each subject needs per day, and the programs in his school. This is a source of tension for him that he is trying to alleviate with the help of his teachers.

Another stressor for Leo is his age. He feels that people do not take him seriously because he has not been in education as long as some of his colleagues. He combats this by listening to his teachers and working with them on issues. He willingly admits his limitations, but he says that his willingness to learn or listen has helped sway a few people's opinions of him in a positive direction.

As an assistant, he has a good relationship with his administrator, but he is not invited to administrative team meetings and has to rely on his principal to give him information about what happened at the meetings. Leo has not had the opportunity to build relationships with other associate principals in the district as they never have meetings. While Leo feels his age is a detriment, he does not have access to the experiences of his colleagues to help him shape his leadership practices.

The support of students outside of the regular education classroom has given Leo a unique perspective when it comes to being part of the leadership team for his school. One priority he has learned from this is the need for clear communication with the students, families, and teachers with whom he works. Leo finds two of his positive tensions revolve around his ability to communicate with staff and how he handles situations.

Leo loves working with and for students, but another of his sources of tension is the school's discipline policy. There are instances when Leo does not agree with the consequences he has to administer, but because they are policies, he needs to follow them. He wants students to be in school as much as possible, so things like suspensions seem counterintuitive to his beliefs. He realizes this is not something he currently has the power to change and that is a source of stress.

CONCLUSION

Tension is often substituted with terms such as *challenges* or *stress*. Challenges imply that something can be overcome and can include: personal challenges, external challenges, emotional challenges, physical challenges, or anything that poses a barrier to accomplishing a task. The term *stress*, on the other hand, tends to refer to what a person feels in reaction to a scenario. A 2017 American Psychological Association (APA) study listed the most common sources of stress among Americans to be the future of our nation (63 percent), money (62 percent), work (61 percent), political climate (57 percent), and violence and crime (52 percent) (APA, 2017, p. 1).

So while they may seem interchangeable, the terms *tension*, *challenge*, and *stress* are different. However, they are symbiotic in nature. Challenges can cause stress, which can in turn create tension-filled situations. The next chapters will delve into the stories of teachers and administrators, providing understanding of the impact of the tension on academic environments as seen in how they utilize positive and negative tensions to foster change in their settings.

Nicole recently completed her nineteenth year as a suburban high school teacher. Nicole comes from a family of educators, which has created her love of learning and teaching. Along with being an educator, Nicole is also active in her district's union, working to foster constant conversations and bridge the communication between the superintendent of the district and the teachers. This position has given her leadership opportunities and created unique tensions.

Nicole has very few tensions, but she broke her tensions down into internal and external. Nicole very much cites her experiences and years in education as a coping mechanism for her tensions and as the reason why she does not experience more of them. The tools that Nicole has in her personal toolkit for dealing with tensions have greatly decreased the tensions she has allowed to impact or bother her over the course of her career. The tensions that she does experience are either a) pressure and stress she puts on herself, or b) new situations within constantly evolving educational systems.

Nicole does not believe that all tensions are bad, but neither did she vocalize that tensions are good. She finds that tension, particularly the tension created internally, spurs action and production. This, she states, is beneficial. In a tense moment, however, she does not care for the feelings associated with those tensions. Nicole's overall stance towards tension is that she approaches the situations with the thoughts or mentality of "what I can control vs. what I cannot" as well as "what I can affect, and what I cannot affect." This helps her decide how she is going to approach the tension.

Nicole's biggest source of tension is grading student assignments with fidelity. She gives feedback, revises and edits, and helps students become stronger communicators with the written word. This, however, causes Nicole to have hours upon hours of grading just about every night. When she assigns a major writing assignment, she has some techniques such as staggering turn-in dates and doing a certain number of papers a night to help her maintain a bit of sanity, but the piles of ever-present, lengthy assignments do take up a lot of her time. Nicole's perspective is this is the profession she chose; she knew what the role entailed.

REFLECTIVE QUESTIONS

1. What creates tension in your setting?
2. What creates tension in your educational environment?
3. Based on the themes presented above, are there certain areas of tension to which you more closely relate?
4. Based on the themes presented above, are there certain areas of tension that you have not experienced?

5. Having read the descriptions of the participants, is there an educator whose beliefs align closely with your own?

REFERENCES

American Psychological Association. (2017). "Stress in America: The State of Our Nation." *American Psychological Association*, November 1, 2017. https://www.apa.org/news/press/releases/stress/2017/state-nation.pdf.

Lehne, Moritz, and Stefan Koelsch. (2015). "Toward a General Psychological Model of Tension and Suspense." *Frontiers in Psychology* 6. https://doi.org/10.3389/fpsyg.2015.00079.

OECD. (2020). *TALIS 2018 Results (Volume II): Teachers and School Leaders as Valued Professionals*. TALIS, OECD Publishing. https://doi.org/10.1787/19cf08df-en.

Quick, Jonathan D., James Campbell Quick, and Debra L. Nelson. (1998). "The Theory of Preventive Stress Management in Organizations." In Cary L. Cooper (ed.), *Theories of Organizational Stress* (pp. 246–248). Oxford University Press.

Chapter 2

Finding the Joy in Our Tensions

INVIGORATION AND TERROR

Entering into your first classroom is an invigorating and terrifying experience wrapped into one moment. To walk into your classroom for the first time is invigorating. The dream of becoming a teacher is now a reality. You have been granted the opportunity to impact the lives of your students that will last a lifetime.

Walking into the classroom for the first time can also be terrifying. While the opportunity to impact the lives of students has been a goal, there may be an underlying fear of "am I good enough to do this?" "I can't believe they (administration) trust me to do this." "What if I screw these kids up?" The competing feelings can be paralyzing as a new teacher scans their new classroom and wonders where to begin.

As the days, weeks, and months pass the work of education begins to consume the efforts of a new teacher, often resulting in working long hours that extend late into the evening and into the weekend. As a recent graduate, the transition to a teaching position feels like you have remained in the teacher preparation program. Reading curriculum, designing lessons and interventions, and late nights are something you have grown accustomed to.

Feeling invigorated is still part of your passion for teaching. The hours and time are worth it. The students are learning. They are engaged. They are experiencing your impact. Turning down social invitations seems okay because this is what teachers do. Teachers give to their students so they can succeed. They just didn't know it would be this much.

This is what makes teachers great: their commitment to other people's kids. It is also what makes the professions so challenging. The commitment to other people's kids can lead to a constant struggle between the time allotted to your personal family and the time allotted to someone else's family. Teachers signed up for the job, but it still hurts when your own child hits their first and only home run in their softball career and you miss it because you are helping someone else's child.

Every educator knows what they signed up for when they entered the profession; in fact, other people's kids are exactly why educators joined the profession. However, when the hours, the workload, expectations, and lack of respect are faced daily, the internal tension can sometimes become unbearable.

Macy has been teaching in the same school for the past eight years. Seven of those years in first grade and one year in kindergarten. In addition to her teaching certification, Macy has a reading license and has recently completed a master's degree in school leadership. Over the past eight years she has met with students and parents who have demanded much of her attention, as well as colleagues who needed her support.

In all of these instances she has reflected on these experiences to learn and grow. Still, she can't help wondering, "Am I doing enough, am I doing my best or should I be taking more home, doing more on the weekends, staying later? Is this what's expected of me or am I putting too much stress on myself? That's the tension, sometimes not knowing if I'm doing enough."

Not knowing if a teacher is doing enough for their students or their administrators adds another layer of tension to their jobs. It creates an internal tension that lives within the core of their being. Not only do they worry about the decisions they make for their students, they also worry about the decisions they make that will create a power struggle between them and their administrator. The balance can become detrimental when the focus is on "not pissing off" an administrator rather than doing what is best for students.

For Delilah, this is something she worries about daily, and in some cases moment by moment. A self-described "people-pleaser," she wants to please her administrator. However, in an effort to please her administrator she finds tension in her struggle. "I think I am constantly thinking about decisions I make in my teaching as well as how I ask for permission on things because I'm worried of the stress or tension between myself and my administrator. So, am I pissing (admin) off and making choices that would not piss (admin) off." Similar to Macy, Delilah wonders if she is doing enough.

Teachers require feedback on their teaching strategies for them to understand if what they are doing is effective and enough for their students. A great deal has been written and studied about the effectiveness of timely giving to students and teachers. The specificity and timeliness of feedback has been proven to improve student learning and teacher effectiveness. For Delilah, the evaluation process was a source of tension. It left her wondering if she was doing enough for her students.

It also left her wondering if she had done enough to please her administrator and avoid a power struggle. "I remember as a first year teacher being scared shitless of (administration) because she'd come in for an observation and it'd be like—I don't even look up, I don't address anyone, and so I remember as a teacher in her building feeling a tension because you didn't always necessarily get positive (feedback) either. It's just who she was and her personality; I remember feeling really anxious, 'Well am I doing the right thing?' 'How do I feel about that?'"

Administrators experience similar feelings of invigoration and terror when assuming their roles of leadership with the organization. Whether an administrator is charged with leading a building or assuming district level responsibilities, the feelings and questions are similar to a teacher's. "Am I good enough to do this?" "I can't believe they (school board) trust me to do this." "What if I screw these kids and teachers up?"

NOT IN TEACHER PREPARATION PROGRAMS

The tensions present in the school are everywhere. Teachers and administrators can experience their own personal tensions. Feelings of inadequacy, strength, intelligence, and passion can all create internal tensions. Expectations and the pace of introducing content can be the cause of tensions between teachers, as well as between teachers and administrators. In the midst of the tensions there can be the overwhelming feeling of "I didn't sign up for this."

So many teachers enter the field to make a difference in the lives of the students. Teachers are humanitarians. They believe in their students and they believe that they are making a difference in their local community and even the entire global community. When they enter the classroom, close the door, and allow their teaching talents to flow, there is nothing that can stop a good teacher from making a positive impact on a student.

A talented kindergarten teacher can have her class on the edge of their seat while she introduces a new topic. Her students hang on to her every word until she finally shares with them what they will be learning. In those moments she has captured the hearts and minds of her students. She has convinced them that learning is worthwhile and, most importantly, that they are learners and are worthy of her time and talent. This is what she dreamed of, worked for, and signed up for.

What she didn't sign up for is all of the other requirements that create internal and external tensions.

How a teacher instructs in the classroom is personal. A delicate balance of science and artistry. A good teacher understands the qualities of a well-designed lesson, classroom management, and the scope and sequence of the curriculum. A great teacher knows all of those things and knows the artistry of performance, engagement, and motivation.

But how many times do the pressures of delivering content in a prescribed manner at the prescribed pace and with the prescribed materials prevent a good teacher from being great? The tension develops when the prescribed curriculum prevents the teacher from doing the job in a manner that is responsive to the needs of their students.

Macy feels this tension as a result of the curriculum and being responsive to students' needs. "I guess it's the needs of the students too; are they ready for this? I guess it goes back to curriculum too, is this curriculum, certain parts of it, responsive to this kid at this time? Because some of it moves in a way that certain kids aren't moving so that's part of that that's hard."

So much research has been conducted on the efficacy of length of lessons, the impact of learning targets posted in the room, teacher talk versus student talk, teacher evaluation, feedback, and so on. It seems just as teachers are comfortable delivering the newest curriculum, administrators make a change due to new research.

While the research on education should not be discounted, the importance of the artistry of how a teacher does their job is lost. It is confusing when administrators ask teachers to follow strict accountability rules, while at the very same time complaining and even fighting against the strict and uniform guidelines required by the district office. In these cases the humanity of teaching is removed from the classroom. The ability to do "the job" or "do the work" is strained.

The mounting requirements that force teachers and administrators to be focused on pace, scope and sequence, and time of lessons at the expense of creating connections and building relationships may leave them conflicted and frustrated. As Macy notes, in the middle of all of this are her students. They have been placed in her care and she has to determine what is the best way to meet their needs while balancing all of the demands placed on her.

> Let's see, that could be one, just not knowing, trying to figure out if there's something more to them (students). Like if students have a processing thing going on and you're trying to figure it out, especially with six- and seven-year-olds. Is this them being defiant or them not truly understanding the question of the book, or—it's always . . . my mind will dart around like, "what is it?" So, that is part of it too. Sometimes it's just their development too; they are very scatter-brained and distracted, and that can make it really hard to teach them too. So . . . yeah, just juggling all those different things.

In the face of all of these challenges, Macy loves coming to school. While it is her job, it is more than that to her. It is her calling and her passion. In her classroom is where she finds her joy.

FINDING AND HOLDING ON TO THE JOY

Speaking of joy in our work can elicit different responses. For some people, talking about the importance of joy in or at work can serve as a distraction from the goals or bottom line of the job. But for many, a joyful workplace serves to increase productivity and create a culture that serves to meet the needs of the employees, as well as the people the organization serves.

For schools, a joyful classroom can lead to improved student achievement, happy teachers, satisfied parents, and proud administrators. Steven Wolk (2008) emphasizes the importance of joy in school this way: "If the experience of 'doing school' destroys children's spirit to learn, their sense of wonder, their curiosity about the world, and their willingness to care for the human condition, have we succeeded as educators, no matter how well our students do on standardized tests?" (p. 8). The same can be attributed to teachers and administrators. If the experience of "doing school" destroys their will to teach, to inspire, and to advocate on behalf of their students, then what good can come of being an educator?

In addition to Wolk's thoughts related to doing school, he identifies a number of focus points for increasing joy in schools:

1. Find the pleasure in learning
2. Give students choice
3. Let students create things
4. Show off student work
5. Take time to tinker
6. Make school spaces inviting
7. Get outside
8. Read good books
9. Offer more gym and arts classes
10. Transform assessment

While the intention of this list can be seen as student focused, it also serves to focus on creating schools that are intent on creating joyful experiences for teachers and administrators. Given the inherent tensions that exist within schools (e.g., to get through the curriculum and make sure we are doing enough for our students), could we meet the needs of our students if we allowed teachers and administrators the time to tinker more. What could happen if teachers and administrators were provided more flexibility by allowing more choice in their daily practices?

In 2007, a small group of educators began meeting as a small group to understand the reasons students in their school were lagging behind in their literacy skills. The group began meeting regularly with the principal as well as the director of curriculum. Much of the agenda for the meetings was created collaboratively between the teaching staff and the administration. Eventually the group settled on the text *Read, Write, Lead* by author Regie Routman to guide their conversations. The discussions lead the group to create a menu of professional development opportunities for staff.

While the menu had a strong literacy focus, it also included professional development for classroom management, the importance of play, project-based learning, and equitable instructional practices among other topics. All professional development sessions were scheduled to meet once a month throughout the course of the school year. Sessions were led by teachers and administrators.

On the surface what this school staff did may not sound groundbreaking. However, the staff reported feeling empowered that they had a voice and choice in the development of professional development. As one teacher said, "I have never had these types of professional discussions with teachers across grade levels about writing. It feels good to have professional discussions about things I'm passionate about."

WILL I EVER GET BETTER?

Many teachers are driven to achieve. Many of them were good students in school and often they report that they have Type A personalities. They are driven to find the best ways to instruct their students in an effort to help their students maximize their learning as well as their students' success. Paula is a middle school teacher with over thirty years of teaching experience. While she has many years of experience, she has stopped wondering if she will ever get better at what she is doing. Instead, she explores what she can do to get better. She has no desire to become complacent. She is driven to provide the best opportunities she can for her students.

Still tensions persist. However, framing the idea of tensions differently can make a significant impact. For Paula it is reframing the idea of tension. "I changed my mind. I think of tensions as all of a sudden you're going to explode. So I changed the word *tension* in my mind to process it better to *challenges*. And then I thought about challenges and changes—that's life. So, you know, that's kind of how I approach it." A simple shift from thinking about tensions to challenges opened her mind to possibilities rather than feeling overwhelmed and ready to explode.

This is the process of getting better. As a teacher or an administrator it's easy to become overwhelmed by all of the tensions that can be experienced. Tensions will never be eliminated. However, building the capacity to manage and reframe tensions can move teachers and administrators forward. Paula did this by changing the word. But what if changing the word tension to another word does not work?

As we move through careers, there are times in which we feel that we have it figured out. The lesson we taught was perfect. The students were engaged, the delivery was exceptional, and the students were able to demonstrate proficiency. Likewise for administrators, feeling like they have figured it out may be the result of an initiative that was implemented with fidelity, a parent conversation that was positive, or an evaluation process that was effective. In those moments we feel like we have figured it out. It's as if we are seeing things in slow motion and we are able to anticipate our next instructional or leadership decision before anyone else.

Being immersed in an activity or topic has been described as flow psychology by Mihaly Csikszentmihalyi. According to Csikszentmihalyi (2008), flow is a state of mind in which a person becomes fully immersed in a topic or activity. Achieving a state of flow is defined by ten characteristics.

1. The activity is intrinsically rewarding.
2. There are clear goals that, while challenging, are still attainable.
3. There is a complete focus on the activity itself.
4. People experience feelings of personal control over the situation and the outcome.
5. People have feelings of serenity and a loss of self-consciousness.
6. There is immediate feedback.
7. People know that the task is doable and there is a balance between skill level and the challenge presented.
8. People experience a lack of awareness of their physical needs.
9. There is strong concentration and focused attention.
10. People experience timelessness, or a distorted sense of time, that involves feeling so focused on the present that you lose track of time passing.

Being in a state of flow is often viewed through the lens of an individual experience. In education a teacher can be in a state of flow while actively delivering a lesson, or while creating a lesson. An administrator can be in a state of flow while conducting a staff meeting or while creating a long-term plan. Students can be in a state of flow while completing an activity or while consuming a lesson presentation. To overcome the tensions that teachers, administrators, and even students can experience, we need to consider how being in a state of flow can intersect across a school.

If the desire is to improve as an educator, how can we leverage the characteristics of flow to maximize our improvement? The first step is to look at those characteristics that are closely connected to education.

The first characteristic: The activity is intrinsically rewarding.

We are asked to complete many tasks within our daily duties. Some we like, some we do not. Nevertheless all the tasks we are asked to complete play a role in the educational system. Whether it is completing an assessment, filling out a report, developing a budget, or counseling a student or staff member, each task is important and critical to the success of the school and the school district.

For Antony, the frustration in many of the tasks he is asked to complete does not always seem to fit into the big picture of education. "I went into education to make a difference. The longer I'm in education . . . it is harder and harder to make a difference. Every year it seems as though making a difference becomes less and less the focus. It's always another initiative. Another version of the resource we've been using. It's frustrating. I want to make my students, my teachers, and my school better. I don't need anyone else to motivate me to do that. It's in me. But I worry that with all of the extra things, it's hard to keep the internal fire going."

Many educators may have similar feelings or experiences as Antony. We entered education to make a difference and there are times when the internal fire may begin to lose some of its light. But the light can be reignited. "If you isolate yourself and become overwhelmed and angry at all of the new things, then motivation wanes. I don't need anyone to motivate me, I want to do well. I want to make a difference. My teachers want to teach and make a difference. When I'm feeling overwhelmed I remember why I began in education. And if that doesn't work, I will visit a kindergarten classroom and those kids will light your fire."

Antony wants to do better because it is in him to want to do better. He is intrinsically motivated and when he is able to focus on those things that are intrinsic, he is able to remember why he is in education and his purpose. It helps him to get better and do better at his job.

While adults may be able to harness their own intrinsic motivation, it becomes a challenge to find ways to help students unleash their intrinsic motivations. Classroom teachers can find it difficult to keep students engaged in the lessons they are presenting to their students when the content, delivery method, and pace are not matching the developmental readiness of their students.

When there is a disconnect between the content that is delivered and the students' willingness to consume the content, the chances for experiencing a state of flow decrease. The competing forces result in teachers relying on external motivation for their students. While external motivation is an effective tool for teachers, when it becomes the preferred method for students to learn, it minimizes the students' ability to develop a lifelong love of learning.

When administrators introduce a new initiative or a teacher presents a lesson to their students, the goals must be clear, challenging, and attainable. When an initiative and lesson have all three of these things, the chances of administrators, teachers, and students experiencing a state of flow increase.

Antony has realized during his career that he has been part of initiatives that have lacked clear, challenging, and attainable goals. As an administrator, he has been guilty of designing new initiatives that lacked one or all of those features. When this has happened, the initiative languishes until it finally slowly, painfully fades away.

> I think early in my career I wanted to find the "silver bullet" that would revolutionize the way we did things and also increase student achievement. So I went looking for programs that promised great success. I finally found a program that I was convinced would do everything I wanted. I bought it and presented it to the teachers. I was young, and I had a veteran staff. They were so kind as they looked at me knowing this would never work. They were right; it didn't work. I didn't have a clear vision. They were talented teachers and I asked them to take the art out of their teaching and implement a prescriptive resource. In the end it was a failure.

Teachers are both masters of the content and artists in the delivery of the content. When either of those two things are removed, or one outweighs the other, the tension that arises prevents teachers from achieving a state of flow. In Antony's situation, he had not created a situation in which the goals were challenging. He implemented a prescribed resource. Unintentionally, he had created a situation in which he undervalued the professional capabilities of his teaching staff. As a result they disengaged from the program, which in turn left the students disengaged. What Antony learned is that there is no silver bullet.

> Reflecting on that experience after a number of years is a bit embarrassing. But I try to remember that we are all learners and that we learn by our mistakes. What I did learn is that I needed to create an environment where we collectively set the goals. Since that time, I believe the best teaching and learning has happened when we set goals that were challenging and that we had developed together. We have not always hit our goals, but we have been more focused and intentional. I also think our teachers and students feel more excited to learn when we have done that.

While experiencing flow within the school and classroom can have an impact in reframing tensions to challenges, the idea of autonomy in a school and a classroom also has an impact on how tensions are perceived and managed. Johnmarshall Reeve and Sung Hyeon Cheon (2016) have explored the idea of autonomy-supportive teaching. Teachers who combine a "students first" perspective and an interpersonal tone of understanding create an environment in which students develop intrinsic motivation and internalization. If an autonomy-supportive teaching style can foster intrinsic motivation and internalization in students, could the same be true if administrators utilized the same framework for their teachers?

An underlying tension from many teachers is the desire for autonomy within their classroom. They desire to be responsive to the needs of their students but often feel conflicted by how they meet the needs of their students. The internal tension may come from administrative pressure to remain on pace with curriculum during the year. Tension may come from knowing their students may not be progressing as they would like and yet teachers may lack the confidence in their own skills to address the needs of their students. This is the case for Delilah.

> I like it when I'm told I have choice in teaching and my students have choice in their learning. It makes sense to me. But sometimes I also feel like I wish I would just be told what to do. When so many of my students have such different needs I worry that if I don't make the right decision I will screw them up. I know I probably won't, but I worry about it.

Teachers worry that making the wrong decisions for their students can have paralyzing effects for teachers. It creates tension that lives within them moment by moment and day by day. They desire the autonomy to meet the needs of their students and adjust the pace and manner in which the content is delivered. When this struggle is living in the teachers, it is the calling of the administrator to support the teachers.

Per Antony,

> I want the teachers I work with to know I trust them to make their own decisions in the classroom. I tell them to meet the needs of their students. But they still struggle in trusting themselves to make those decisions. I think the inability for them to trust themselves is in part due to administrators. We give too many conflicting messages.
>
> We will tell teachers to be responsive to the needs of their students and then cringe if a classroom is behind on pace. We tell teachers to focus on student growth, but then cringe when the students grow, but not as much as the experts told us they should grow. As administrators we need to listen to our teachers and

then adjust based on what they are telling us. We need to trust them. They are experts in the room. They want to do well. We need to trust them and support them to do well.

The tensions are numerous and they have the capacity to weigh teachers and administrators down. However, if teachers and administrators are provided the opportunity to view tensions as challenges, change can happen. Teachers and administrators can get better when they take a student focus first, and a teacher focus first approach. They can create a learning environment that focuses on professional autonomous decision-making. When this is done, students, teachers, and administrators can experience flow while internalizing their intrinsic motivation to learn and improve.

YES . . . THIS IS ALL WORTH IT

"I went into education for the money, respect, and admiration of others." Unfortunately, this is not a sentence many educators often say or even can say. The climate in our society today is not educator friendly. The increasing demands placed on administrators to ensure high standardized test scores make for challenging school days. Teachers are increasingly tasked with teaching more while getting no more additional time to teach. Additionally, classroom teachers are now not just teachers but counselors, social workers, advisors, and friends. All of these demands create an environment that is rife with tension.

When we are tense, we can overlook the happiness that is right in front of us: our students. The students are why we went into education. We entered into education to make their lives better so that society could be better for all. No one really told us the tensions that would ensue. If they did, we did not listen. We were convinced that we would make a difference. We would not let stress and the demands of the job affect us. Soon we found that we were human. We experienced the same tensions as those before us. But there is a path up to making it all worth it, and that path is through happiness.

As educators it can become easy to get lost in the stress and the tensions of the day. But what if we pushed back against the tensions and the stress and instead focused on happiness. In Shawn Achor's book *The Happiness Advantage* (2010), he writes about falling up. "The most successful decisions come when we are thinking clearly and creatively enough to recognize all the paths available to us, and accurately predict where the path will lead. The problem is when we are stressed or in crisis, many people miss the most important path of all: the path up" (p. 108).

Finding the path up, to the path that we know what we do is worth it, means we must focus on our mindset in spite of the tensions that are in front of us. The content may not change, the pacing may not slow down, and the needs of our teachers and students may not lessen, but our perception of turning what is happening to us into what we can make out of what happened can help us find the path up to "it is worth it."

Educators are investors in social capital. They believe in people and they believe that what they do matters and they make a difference. However, even investors in social capital can sometimes wonder if the investment is paying off. When things get tense and stress runs high, even the strongest of educators can retreat to isolation and shame that they have not been able to figure it out on their own. There is vulnerability in admitting that help is needed. For Antony, it's really hard.

> There is such pressure as an administrator to have all of the answers. When I'm fielding so many questions in a day I can become paralyzed with my own thoughts. I have to make the right decision. The stress can be overwhelming. Thank God I have people who will kick me in the ass and remind me I don't have to be the smartest person in the room.
>
> When I take a deep breath and talk to others we make better decisions. When I started I felt like I had to make every decision and if I asked for help I would look incompetent. I've come to learn that's not the case. We want our kids to collaborate and ask for help and yet we are not always great at trusting ourselves to collaborate.

As Antony describes his growth and willingness to invite people into the decision-making process, it has had an effect on his happiness and has reduced his tensions. He admits it took him some time to get to that point. It has made him a more collaborative leader, although he recognizes he still needs work in the area of collaboration. What Antony has experienced is directly connected to the social investment that he has made in his teachers and his students. It has been a challenging transformation, but it has been worth it.

Finding the worth in what educators do is personal for every educator. For some, finding worth means a defined percentage of their students passed the advanced placement exam. For some, it means that the students in their class have high engagement during their lessons. For others, it is the note that they receive from a student years after they have been in their class. In whatever manner educators find worth in their jobs, they do so through a spirit of resilience. In the ever-changing political influences placed on educators, their job is to make sure their students learn and are taken care of. They must have resilience, model resilience, and teach resilience.

In recent years resilience has become the focus in books like *Grit* by Angela Duckworth (2017). Grit is defined as a positive, noncognitive trait based on a person's perseverance combined with their passion for a goal. To be a teacher, having grit helps. In fact, Angela Duckworth found that "optimistic teachers were grittier and happier, and grit and happiness explained why optimistic teachers got their students to achieve more during the school year" (p. 177). Teachers can overcome the tensions when they know that what they do is worth it and makes a difference in the lives of their students.

As Paula notes: "I see the obstacles as challenges. I keep teaching because I believe in what I do. I want my students to have a good experience. I have to give them a good experience so they will be able to overcome challenges and take care of themselves later in life." Paula is optimistic and believes that the tensions in her life represent the challenges she is teaching her students to overcome. Her belief in her students and what she teaches lets her students know they are worth it and, in turn, she knows everything she does for them is worth it.

REFLECTIVE QUESTIONS

1. What parts of your job do you find invigorating?
2. What sorts of activities might your group feel empowered by?
3. How could you define the "worth" in what you do educationally?

REFERENCES

Achor, Shawn. (2010). *The Happiness Advantage: The Seven Principles of Positive Psychology That Fuel Success and Performance at Work.* Crown Publishing Group.

Csikszentmihalyi, Mihaly. (2008). *Flow: The Psychology of Optimal Experience.* Harper Perennial Modern Classics.

Duckworth, Angela. (2017). *Grit: Why Passion and Resilience Are the Secrets to Success.* Vermilion.

Reeve, Johnmarshall, and Cheon, Sung Hyeon. (2016). "Teachers Become More Autonomy Supportive After They Believe It Is Easy to Do." *Psychology of Sport and Exercise* 22: 178–189.

Routman, Regie. (2014). *Read, Write, Lead: Breakthrough Strategies for Schoolwide Literacy Success.* ASCD.

Wolk, Steven. (2008). "Joy in School." *Educational Leadership* 66(1): 8–15.

Chapter 3

When Organizational Tensions Affect Culture

The daily responsibilities of administrators and teachers are numerous: focusing on the consistency of content delivery to students, lesson planning, school-wide and classroom behavior management, and other tasks like making sure the busses arrive on time, lunch is served on time, and there is soap in the soap dispenser.

In isolation, few of these tasks may seem like they can have a significant impact on students and their ability to learn. However, collectively each of these tasks, along with many others, can impact the environment of a school and a whole district positively and negatively. Depending on the responsibilities assigned to administrators, as well as teachers, tensions can develop that have an impact on students.

All of the responsibilities assigned to administrators and teachers are critical to ensure that a school is safe and the needs of the students are addressed. One assigned responsibility that is not often specifically assigned is the establishment of a positive school culture. Tensions impact the creation and continued perpetuation of school culture, both positive and negative. Kent Peterson and Terrence Deal in their book *Shaping School Culture: The Heart of Leadership* (2010) note that school culture is a set of values, norms, celebrations, and traditions that establish the way a school operates. In many ways, school culture is defined as the way things are done in the school.

Determining if a school culture is positive or negative can be done by assessing the underlying assumptions of students, professional development, and what is discussed at meetings. In a negative school culture, the underlying tone is that the students are incapable of success, relationships between staff members are prone to conflict, and staff do not have the belief that they can achieve their vision. In a positive school culture, there is shared commitment to student success, professional development that improves teacher practices, and a positive and caring atmosphere between students and staff.

Many schools and districts focus much of the professional development activities on understanding new content standards and the associated teaching practices on how to deliver the standards. The focus on student performance on standardized tests and the pressure to perform in the public spotlight has resulted in the focus on school culture being an afterthought. The collective work of researchers and authors like Peterson, Deal, Whitaker, Gruenert, and others all show that a focus on establishing a positive school culture has a greater impact on students and teachers than most other initiatives.

Instead of making culture a focus, the day-to-day pressures of improving standardized test scores overshadows the development of a positive school culture. The tension experienced by administrators, teachers, and students to perform is overwhelming. However, could tension to perform be leveraged to create a positive school culture and thereby improve leadership, teaching, practices, and student achievement?

ADMINISTRATOR RESPONSIBILITIES

A major responsibility of a district-level or building-level administrator is to ensure that the academic programming is implemented consistently and with fidelity throughout the district and within individual classrooms. As part of that responsibility, there are times in which a building principal may have to coach staff members to move forward when they are opposed to portions of the academic program. For Matt, this was a real challenge with one of his veteran teachers.

> I have a teacher that is adamant that cursive writing (be taught) and it is something that as a district we've moved away from, but this individual just does not want to let that (cursive) go. She's been utilizing literacy time to focus on teaching cursive. She and I had some conversations about teaching cursive at that time. If she wants to teach cursive writing during some free time, I can support the use of that time. However, when we're stealing time from universal instruction to focus on cursive writing that creates some challenges.

On the surface, this is a tension that most administrators will experience at least once during their career. However, it is indicative of the tensions that are present as part of an administrator's responsibilities. It is the constant balance of the daily grind and establishing a strong culture that provides the foundation for every decision made in the school.

While the role of the school administrator is varied, the most important focus should be on culture building. For many administrators the way in which to establish a strong school culture is to focus on establishing positive relationships between staff, students, and with the community. For students, this is established by feeling part of the classroom community. For teaching staff, it is feeling supported and having a sense of autonomy in their classroom. For parents, it is having good communication and being kept informed by the administrator.

In order to keep all three stakeholders engaged in the school, the principal must build relationships. Shelly Habegger writes about the power of relationships in her article "The Principal's Role in Successful Schools: Creating a Positive School Culture" (2008). Specifically, she notes that successful schools have principals who are able to multitask while never losing sight of the importance of establishing a positive school culture. In the most successful schools, the principals create and facilitate school environments in which students feel a sense of belonging.

When students feel as if they belong, they are more likely to come to school. Likewise, teachers require a sense of belonging while also feeling as though they are treated as professionals. In the most successful schools, teachers experience a sense of autonomy when they are part of a team that is allowed to make educational decisions based on the needs of their students. Finally, in the most successful schools, principals solicit and accept feedback from parents based on their needs and the needs of their students. Principals in successful schools listen and learn from the community, and develop a partnership with the parents of their students.

The challenge for principals is managing all of the responsibilities while still devoting the necessary time and resources to changing the culture of a building. Mitch experienced the challenges of shifting culture in his high school.

> I started the change in culture with the department chairs. When I started the meetings were pretty procedural, they (the department chairs) weren't really leading. They were doing the budget; they were doing the scheduling. So we held a department chair retreat prior to the second school year when we're going to lay out the vision of what we are going to do for the next ten years. I put it out there to them saying I need you to be the change agents and the leaders in your department because it just can't come from the administrative team.

At the time Mitch started the process of establishing his culture, he gave permission to his department chairs to begin making decisions that would align with the vision they had collectively established at their retreat. While this process felt good to start, it was not without tension.

> I think as a new principal in a building, particularly someone who is following a principal who had been here for twenty-one years, there were some shifts in philosophies that had to happen, you know. And, you come into a staff that has

been used to one philosophy and when that philosophy shifts slightly that can cause some tensions—particularly, I think, given the age dynamic as well.

Being a young principal, and some of the stereotypes of a young principal and the motives, sometimes I think there's a thought that the young principal is going to come in and try to make their impact as a way to climb, rather than necessarily having the best interest of the students or the school or the staff in mind.

Here lies a tension for Mitch. The responsibility to transform and lead his staff to benefit the students, while trying to reduce the concern that he is using this position as a stepping stone.

While Mitch and Matt both experience tension while trying to create a positive culture within the school, they both have the responsibility to implement systemic initiatives that have been mandated by the district. Both agree that having consistency in academic programming throughout the district, especially for Matt who is one of five elementary principals, the uniform methodology is not always accepted by the staff.

Frustration can grow when it appears there is inequitable allocation of resources between buildings. There is tension created between administrators and buildings when resources provided to buildings or programs are distributed equally versus equitably. When this happens, Matt recognizes that he must balance the needs of his students against the needs of other students in his district. This is difficult, because in the end "all of the students are our students."

The tensions, and even competition, for resources between buildings or programs within a district can result in disparities between groups of students or between buildings. However, the tensions that develop as a result of securing resources does not always lead to winners and losers. Administrators who develop a method to work collaboratively in order to make decisions about shared resources find that tensions can still be present but that the outcome ultimately benefits students. This has been the experience for Antony.

> There was a time in which we would be invited to a meeting and be told how many new staff we could add across the district. Instead of thinking collaboratively, it became a battle royale. Whoever spoke the loudest and the longest won and the others lost. It led to so much tension, you could cut it with a knife.

After time, Antony said he and his other administrators began to talk and share what each other needed. They all realized that the tension about allocation of resources was creating tension. The tension was so great that it was damaging the relationships among the administrators, between buildings, and the tension was ultimately impacting students. It was when the team realized the negative impact the competition over resources was having that they decided to make a change.

The competition for resources is not unique to educational settings. Businesses and nonprofit groups all have to manage and determine how the resources for the organization will be allocated. What can have an impact on the tension level is how the organizational structure is designed to support and facilitate the process of resource allocation. In some cases this begins with how organizations think differently about the process. In his book *Think Again* (2021), Adam Grant shares how a group of misfits and disagreeable collaborators at Pixar established a "challenge network."

Having disagreeable members of the team should not be interpreted as meaning the members of this group are out looking for conflict or to create tension. The members of the challenge network are not afraid to question the process or the thinking of other members of the group. In order to create an effective challenge network, the organizational culture must have trust and safety so that a free exchange of dialogue and ideas can be shared without personal attacks. What resulted at Pixar was a number of groundbreaking and profitable motion pictures.

The transition in Antony's district was not the formulation of a challenge network, but an organic shift from fighting for resources to a collaborative approach to allocating resources.

> I think we all got tired of fighting. I hated those meetings. They were so toxic and the meetings left so many bad feelings. Eventually, I wish I could say it was me, but it wasn't, one of our members said enough is enough. She proposed that we meet prior to the meeting as principals and discuss our needs openly. It was tough at first but what resulted was so much better. We gained a better understanding of the needs of other buildings. In some cases other buildings gave up resources to help another building. It was amazing. We left feeling like we had made a difference.

To get to the point where Antony and his colleagues were able to have discussions about resource allocation in this manner took time; they needed to rebuild trust. Their efforts created a culture in which they could challenge each other. They had been living in an organization in which tensions were high and they recognized the tensions were having a negative impact on their relationships, their staff, and most importantly their students. Collectively, they leveraged the negative tensions and created a culture that harnessed tension into positive change. "It was not easy. But it was worth it."

Having the courage to name the problem as one of Antony's colleagues did to resolve the toxicity of resource allocation meetings resulted in sustainable change. Naming the problem or the tension is not something that is often done. In many instances, when the problem or the tension is named, there can be resistance to accepting the named tension.

In their book *All In* (2012), Adrian Gostick and Chester Elton discuss the impact of organizational cultures and the importance of recognizing the existence of tension. When an organizational structure does not value the input of the members, the concerns raised can be dismissed. Often noting that the "complainer" represents a lone view, Gostick and Elton posit that the complainer may actually be the person who has the courage to speak up.

Instead of dismissing the concerns, the leader of the organization may want to question why the complaint is being made. Being open to concerns and critique can help establish a culture that encourages questions and critique when the intent of the questions and critique is on improving the organization.

The responsibility to question practices or critique processes should not be limited to individual teachers. Establishing an open and trusting culture means that the school leader must not have a stranglehold on their beliefs. The administrator should understand their beliefs within the context of the vision and mission of the school. As Gostick and Elton note:

> The leader that holds most dearly to the unbreakable nature of their belief is the one I am most worried about, for that pride gets projected in the name of righteousness.
>
> Most problems around promoting shared belief in organizations come from this subtle misguidedness—where we attempt to change others' beliefs while holding on to the supremacy of our own. (p. 33)

When everyone has strong beliefs, the tension present between administrators, or between administrators and teachers, there could be a fear of challenging those beliefs. If a teacher will not speak up because they believe their concerns will not be heard or integrated, then transparent communication cannot occur. Instead, the noise of dialogue becomes deafening silence.

TEACHER RESPONSIBILITIES

Within the organizational structure of the school the responsibility of the teacher is to deliver the curricular content with fidelity. There is much more to being a teacher, but content delivery and student achievement is the foundation of what they are expected to accomplish. For Delilah, how the organization makes decisions about curriculum creates tension for her.

> Curriculum. Ugh! Part of the tension with curriculum is being forced to use a new curriculum that is very guided. The tension comes from the decision-making

process and feeling a little slighted. It feels like they (admin) are saying "your team's not doing well enough." That's my own interpretation because no one ever said anything like that, but we have been told we have to follow it (curriculum resource) verbatim.

From Delilah's viewpoint, the curricular decisions are made unilaterally, with little input from staff. If this is the case, the organizational structure of the school or district is creating, perhaps unintentionally, tensions for teachers. The tensions live in feelings of not being valued, or trusted in making decisions for their students. When this tension exists, it interferes with the establishment of a positive culture.

The feeling of being undervalued has a significant impact on Delilah and her ability to perform her job. She found herself questioning her every decision and it was making her wonder if she wanted to remain in the classroom.

> To be told you have to teach this way has been very hard for me as a teacher. I've researched and put some really strong practices in place and now to have them say, "Yeah, you've done good research and we like what you're doing but we're going to actually tell you what practices we actually want you to put in place" is devastating.
>
> So that curriculum, that guided curriculum is creating a lot of stress and anxiety in my life. I have to find this balance between what I am doing that's right for my students, what I am doing that I fully believe in curricular-wise, and yet I still have to follow what the district's telling me they believe in. And I don't believe that my current views match the district. So that part has been really hard.

The tension for Delilah is growing and she feels trapped.

School cultures vary in the level of positivity. In Delilah's case she does feel as though she can talk to her principal but she feels as conflicted. The organizational structure is designed so that curricular decisions are made at a district level. She does not feel as though the organizational structure is inherently flawed.

Delilah's tension comes from feeling as though her ability to teach is being limited and her expertise is not being considered as part of this change.

> This change has impeded me doing my best. I am constantly asking how do I follow a program that I know right now is not the best for my students? How am I getting to know the program so I can try to find how it can be the best for my students? How am I giving it enough attention but then finding my own personal voice in this curriculum? So right now I am not feeling like I'm being the best teacher that I can be because the curriculum's like impeding me from doing that.

While Delilah focuses much of her energy on the curriculum and how that impacts her ability to teach, it seems as though she is also struggling with being minimized as a teacher and a professional. When she feels this tension, how does this impact her influence on the school culture and what role can one teacher play in shaping school culture?

Often the responsibility of building a positive school culture is assigned to the principal and the leadership team. School culture cannot be the sole responsibility of administrators; teachers have a role in fostering a positive school culture even when they do not have an official leadership title. It has taken time and experience, but for Nicole, she has realized she can be a part of creating a culture of trust when she takes ownership in the day-to-day activities of her school.

> So, I think one of the things that comes with time and experience is knowing what I can affect, and what I can change and what I can't. The things I feel like I can affect change. I guess I try to have those conversations with the people who are the players at the table. Knowing that a lot of times those systems are in place and have been for a long time. They don't change quickly or easily. Sometimes changing one system just brings up another, so maybe, for example, going back to when we changed our schedule and recognizing there is no perfect schedule.

> So even those things that are tricky with the new schedule—I accept because I know the change was made collaboratively. I also know the change was made to help students. So the little things that are tricky for me are worth it because what we changed had a positive change in our students.

Nicole recognized that her responsibility extended beyond the classroom. She could have made the choice to stay within her classroom walls, deliver content, and focus all of her attention on the students she sees everyday. However, she wanted to have a greater impact. She decided to take a seat at the table. She listened and asked questions. She then talked to her colleagues that were skeptical about the change in schedule. She was not able to answer all of her colleagues' concerns, but she could answer many.

Through the process, she felt as though she was being valued as a professional and that her views were heard and accepted. Because of this, her school has transformed itself into one of the highest rated high schools in the region. Most importantly, the students in her school are excelling socially and academically.

The stories of the administrators and teachers illustrate the importance of building a community on trust, communication, and collaboration. In many of the stories, there have been tensions that have been allowed to grow either due to the organizational structure of the school or district or the internal tensions of trying to meet the needs of students. In every case, the administrators or teacher made a purposeful decision to attack the tension.

The core reason for attacking the tension was to change the impact on students. This was not easy and often caused additional stress or consternation for the administrator or the teacher. When the tension was addressed, it not only had a positive impact on the students, but it also had a positive impact on the school culture. In every case, there was improved communication, collaboration, and professional trust between administrators and teachers increased.

Recognizing the organizational flaws within a school or a district takes courage and a willingness to commit the time and energy to challenge the organizational structure. Mary Davenport, in her article "Building a Positive Staff Culture Takes Work" (2008), addresses the issue of time and commitment. Effective teaching is built on a positive relationship between the students and their teacher.

The same is true for school staff. If the staff of a school has positive and trusting relationships among themselves, the school has a greater likelihood of increasing teacher efficacy and student achievement (Peterson and Deal, 2010). Small acts of potluck lunches, social gatherings outside of school (that do not always involve alcohol), and professional development opportunities that focus on self-care and are facilitated by staff have tremendous impact on building the function of a strong school culture.

LEGAL REQUIREMENTS, LOCAL MANDATES, AND STUDENT DISCIPLINE

Potlucks, social gatherings, and surprise jeans days can have an impact on creating a positive school culture, but unfortunately, they do little to reduce the number of legal requirements or mandates that have been assigned to schools, administrators, students, and teachers. The legal requirements and mandates assigned to school are not new. Throughout history, when society has experienced a conflict or identified a need, those needs have been addressed in school.

Thomas Jefferson himself opined that public education was to create an informed electorate so that they may be able to fully participate in the democracy and voting process. Throughout the years, little by little the focus of public education has expanded well beyond educating and informing the electorate.

As public education has continued to evolve, so has federally regulated law. The Equal Protection Clause of the Fourteenth Amendment, the National School Lunch Act, the Bilingual Education Act, Title IX, Equal Educational Opportunities Act of 1974, Family Education Rights and Privacy Act, the

Education for All Handicapped Children Act, and No Child Left Behind have resulted in improved access and services to students and families.

The introduction of many, if not all, of these laws have also reflected the advocacy and societal conditions of the time in which the laws were enacted. The changes in the standards and curriculum that are taught in public schools are a living history of what the local school boards, state governments, and federal government have valued locally and nationally.

The legal requirements and mandates that have been enacted to ensure a free and appropriate public education for all children has not been without tension. Many of the laws and requirements have been vigorously debated, supported, and opposed. One does not have to search long to learn the tension and conflict that resulted in violence during the desegregation of schools. The tension and conflict that happen out in the community also enter the doors of the schoolhouse.

Teachers, administrators, parents, and students may have differing viewpoints on the merits of certain legal requirements or mandates. When a teacher or administrator is opposed to the foundation of a legal decision or mandate, they experience internal, and sometimes external, conflict on how to implement the decision. In most instances, however, the tension ensues when the interpretation of the law is more focused on the rigidity of the law rather than the spirit of the law.

Jeff describes himself as an easygoing person. He enjoys teaching high school students in his rural school district. He has positive relationships with his colleagues and respects the leadership of his building principal. What causes him tension in his environment is the handling of learning for students with a special education need.

> One of the things that causes me the most tension is the different ways to go about business for students with a special education need. I'm sure our program works similarly to other schools. Students with disabilities are included in class and most of the time there is an aide to support the student. In some cases, students are pulled out for tests or help with a project or assignment. Sometimes I wonder what happens when the students are pulled out of the classroom.
>
> For example, when I give a test, the student has accommodations. If I give a test on geography I may have the student only identify the country on a map. I won't require identification of capitals. Over the years, I've learned that students are allowed to use atlases to complete the test. I'm frustrated by this; I don't believe it's fair to them or their learning. I've tried to ask questions about this and it's always met with the same answer, that the kids are allowed this accommodation.

The tension lives in the interpretation of the legal requirement and the assigned accommodation. In the end, Jeff has felt frustrated with the lack of agreement between what is an appropriate accommodation and the student's learning. In the end, he is left feeling as if he is the "bad guy" because he is questioning his colleagues' practices.

These are the tensions that live in schools. The conflicts that occur between what is best for students. Different interpretations of what students need and how instruction should be delivered. In Jeff's case, his tension leaves him wondering if he is the "bad guy" when he believes he is advocating for students. Likewise, the assumption is that the teachers who are in conflict with Jeff also believe they are advocating on behalf of the students and may be experiencing the same level of tension and frustration as Jeff.

This leaves teachers and administrators on their own to make what they believe are the best decisions for their students. However, a positive school culture grounded in professional trust and communication can overcome the tensions created by legal requirements, local mandates, and student discipline.

Tensions between educators are not limited to legal requirements related to students with special education needs. As noted earlier, rules related to funding as well as disbursement of those funds can create tension. In some cases, the tension can happen between classroom teachers, intervention teachers, and special education teachers. There are situations in which students require additional support whether in their home classroom or within a small group outside of their home classroom. For example, a student who may need additional intervention to grow in their reading skills may or may not require services from a special education teacher.

In some cases, the legal requirements limit who may provide the services to the student. If the student requires intervention, an interventionist may provide the support. If the student has an identified learning disability, then a special education teacher is obligated to provide that support.

But what happens when the schedule of the school creates potential issues with how services are provided? What happens when the most qualified teacher to provide the instruction to a student is not a teacher who has the legal obligation to provide the service? In cases such as these the teachers are left to determine how the student's need will be met while living within the confines of the legal requirement or mandate.

The intent for all educators is to do whatever they can in order to provide the best learning environment they can for their students. When there are limits on how the services can be provided, it creates inefficiencies in the delivery of services. This leaves teachers, administrators, parents, and most importantly students feeling frustrated.

When the legal requirements and mandates create barriers, educators who are unwilling to deny students services may choose to bend the rules in the favor of the student. While these efforts are admirable, the actions may result in legal challenges or reprimand from superiors. The positive impact of the tensions in these situations is that solutions can be found when the culture is focused on doing what is best for students as well as trusting communication.

Tensions are also present for administrators when trying to serve and assist teachers in their professional growth and development. For many principals, they will evaluate teaching staff in areas that they may not have specific expertise. A high school principal cannot be an expert in teaching Algebra 2, Chemistry, Art, and Spanish IV, and yet they are assigned with the duty to observe and evaluate teachers. Some elementary principals may not have limited classroom teaching experience. As Regie Routman addresses in her book *Read, Write, Lead* (2014), many elementary principals lack the instructional expertise in the area of literacy for which they are assigned to lead.

This is the very case for Leo, an assistant principal in an elementary school. His background is in special education where he served as an aide. Later he earned a master's degree in counseling and then earned his certification in administration. He feels as though he has a good background in education, but not having specific instructional experience makes him acutely aware of the gaps within his knowledge base.

> I have to do a lot of learning. I feel like my job right now is 100 percent learning. I am slowly getting more exposed to those things (reading, writing, and math) but I also recognize that's not going to be my strength. I worry that because those areas are not my strength that some people may feel that I'm sloughing it off.

There is tension in Leo's story. He recognizes his weaknesses and this causes him stress and tension. He worries that his staff may think he is sloughing off, but he has decided to leverage the tension he feels as motivation to do the work.

> I've taken a few literacy classes and seminars. I've also decided to educate myself in the foundational math instructional techniques. I also know that when I take classes I gain background, but I also don't live that every single day. I can't speak to reading and math scientifically. I have to decide what I need to know and who I need to talk to. That's really going to be able to help our teachers. I rely on our instructional coaches to be the experts and to explain the science behind reading and math. I may not be the expert in those areas, but I am smart enough to know my job is to put people in that position to do that.

Instead of wallowing in the tension of feeling underprepared to be the assistant principal, he leveraged his tension to learn more and to seek the assistance of the experts in his building.

These subtle changes have allowed him to improve his evaluation and observation practices. He feels as though he has developed enough knowledge to have intentional conversations with his staff. He also believes that by being vulnerable and letting his staff know what he needed to learn, he was able to build stronger relationships. His vulnerability empowered other staff members to be vulnerable in a safe and trusting culture. The tension he once felt has yielded a culture in which learning and growing together is now just a "way we do things around here."

Legal requirements and state and local mandates can all have an effect on manufacturing tension. Another organizational structure that can create tension within a school is related to student discipline. Specifically, the way in which it is perceived to be handled or not handled. Todd Whitaker writes in his book *What Great Teachers Do Differently* (2015) that it is not about what happens in the principal's office when a student is sent down to be disciplined but what happens after the student leaves the principal's office. "Effective teachers understand that what matters is not whether a student leaves the office mad, and not what the student reports to his peers, but how the student behaves in the future" (p. 27).

When a student is sent to the office the transgression that has occurred is usually a culmination of events, or a singular major event. In most cases, the teacher has attempted everything in their toolbox to correct the behavior, with limited or no success. The tension is high and the principal's office is the last resort to correcting the behavior.

The tension that results from issues related to student behavior can devastate the culture of a school. Situations in which the teaching staff and principal do not share the same beliefs can negatively affect not only the culture of the school but the manner in which the students are treated during the day. For Macy, the tension lives in what she feels is unclear expectations for student behavior and that her administrator does not seem to share the same concern.

> I think my administrator could benefit from knowing that people don't always understand things the same way that they do. That yeah, one of the things that's been a tension in our building is that people aren't on the same page with behaviors and that's important in a school. So, like one teacher might expect this out at recess and another teacher doesn't; they expect something else. Or even in the hallway you know in the lunchroom and it's important to have everyone on the same page. I don't know if we're quite there yet.

Not being quite there yet leaves Macy feeling confused as to what the expectations are for her students. In situations similar to Macy, some school-wide behavior plans become prescriptive in nature. Each offense has an assigned consequence. In some situations there is little room for investigation or debate. This too creates tension, because it removes the opportunity for learning, conversation, and context between teacher and student, student and principal, and principal and teacher for why the behavior occurred.

In order to move beyond a prescriptive approach to discipline, principals must be willing to communicate completely with teachers when a student is disciplined. Many students, when returned from the principal's office to the classroom, will report that "nothing happened." If the principal does not share with the teacher what did happen, the teacher is left feeling unsupported, frustrated, and filled with tension. This was something Antony had to learn the hard way, early in his career.

> When I became principal, I could be easily manipulated by five- and six-year-olds. They made my heart melt when they cried because they were in trouble. So I ended up consoling them, and telling them not to do whatever they had done again. Then I would send them back to the classroom. This did not go over well with teachers. The kids told them nothing happened. Now I would follow up with parents, but I did not talk to the teachers. I've since learned I have to communicate with the teachers, or they lose faith in how we support them when they send kids to the office.

In Antony and Macy's case, they do not always agree with how things were handled with a student, but because the culture allows for reflection and communication regarding student discipline they are able to leverage the tensions they feel to have a positive impact on students and the building culture. When they communicate with the principal or other teachers, they gain perspective, are able to problem solve, and as Todd Whitaker says: "When a student misbehaves, the great teacher has one goal: to keep the behavior from happening again" (p. 25).

Tensions are going to be present within the organizational structure of an educational system. The hierarchical nature will have people in charge who make decisions that may not be universally accepted by all members of the organization. In effective organizations, the teachers and administrators recognize the tensions and work to leverage the tension for a positive result.

It is easy work to recognize and complain about the tensions in an organization. The real work happens when a group of people engage in trusting dialogue that is focused on improving the organization for students and staff. It does not matter the curriculum, the resources, or the quality of facilities that a school system has; if the system does not have a strong positive culture, the tensions will rule the organization.

REFLECTIVE QUESTIONS

1. In what ways have the tension you experienced encouraged you to be vulnerable in your lack of knowledge and helped you grow as an individual and professional?
2. What structures are in place in your school/district that promote a positive school culture?
3. How have you leveraged the tensions you feel in your organization to make positive change?

REFERENCES

Davenport, Mary. (2008). "Building a Positive Staff Culture Takes Work." *Edutopia*. https://www.edutopia.org/article/building-positive-staff-culture-takes-work.

Gostick, Adrian, and Chester Elton. (2012). *All In: How the Best Managers Create a Culture of Belief and Drive Big Results*. Free Press.

Grant, Adam. (2021). *Think Again: The Power of Knowing What You Don't Know*. Viking Publishing.

Gruenert, Steve, and Todd Whitaker. (2015). *School Culture Rewired: How to Define, Assess, and Transform It*. ASCD.

Habegger, Shelly. (2008). "The Principal's Role in Successful Schools: Creating a Positive School Culture." *Principal* 88(1): 42–46.

Peterson, Kent, and Terrence Deal. (2010). *Shaping School Culture: The Heart of Leadership*. Jossey-Bass Education.

Routman, Regie (2014). *Read, Write, Lead: Breakthrough Strategies for Schoolwide Literacy Success*. ASCD.

Whitaker, Todd (2015). *What Great Teachers Do Differently: 17 Things That Matter Most* (2nd ed.). Routledge.

Chapter 4

What We Wish Administrators Knew

When asked the question, "What do you wish your administrator knew?" Nicole could not think of anything she wanted her administrator to know. She felt that her principal was supportive and empathetic. Even when prompted about her nemesis, grading, and asked if there was anything she wanted her principal to know, she replied, "He already knows." Nicole's situation was unique among the participants who were interviewed for this book.

Unfortunately, this was not the case for all the teachers we talked to. Whether it was because of their own reluctance or because they had already shared these thoughts to no avail, these are the things they wished their administrators knew. These are the things that exacerbated the negative tensions the teachers felt: time crunches, lack of information, and inconsistencies to name a few. The responses, it turns out, mirror themes found throughout education in general and our teachers' thoughts gave deeper insights into these issues.

First, let us look at the relationship between administrators and their teachers. The number of teachers in public and private schools outnumbers principals. An Institute of Education Sciences (IES 2019) analysis during the 2017–2018 school year found there were 3.5 million public school teachers and 90,900 public school principals—a ratio of 38.5 teachers to every one principal.

Imagine running a building of forty educated adults with varying skills, experiences, interests, and needs. How can the relationship between a principal and *each* teacher be harnessed to create an environment conducive to strong teacher and learning experiences? And what is the desired relationship between principal and teacher? Is it boss–employee? Is it one of equal partners? Is it simply leader and follower? Regardless of the leadership style exhibited by the principal, the effects of this relationship impact not only teachers and their administrators, but students, parents, and all stakeholders in a school community.

In order to see teachers' responses through a wider lens than just their own school settings, this chapter uses as the foundation a 2021 study completed by Jason Grissom, Anna Egalite, and Constance Lindsay for the Wallace Foundation: "How Principals Affect Students and Schools: A Systematic Synthesis of Two Decades of Research" (Grissom, Egalite, and Lindsay 2021). This and other works will help to create a picture of how the data mined from our teachers gives specific terms such as care, communication, trust, and undiscussables that can be used to possibly relieve some of the negative tensions educators face.

Grissom, Egalite, and Linsday's synthesis of previous research found three areas that administrators need to be competent in if they are to be successful in their roles:

- Instruction
- People
- The Organization

Once the data from the teachers interviewed were analyzed, three themes emerged:

- Know That Your Teachers' Time with Students Is Valuable
- Know Your Teachers
- Know Your Expectations Have Been Understood

And when the data from both are put together, the results show strikingly similar categories for both as seen in Table 4.1. Let us delve into each of these.

INSTRUCTION: KNOW THAT TEACHERS' TIME WITH STUDENTS IS VALUABLE

Ariel wants her administrators to know that the smallest change in the routine or schedule has a huge impact on the day. She says these little changes have

Table 4.1 Principal Competency Skills versus Teacher Interview Category Alignment

Grissom et al. Principal Competency Skills	Teacher Interview Category Alignment: What Do You Want Your Administrator to Know?
Instruction	Know That Teachers' Time with Students Is Valuable
People	Know Your Teachers
The Organization	Know That Your Expectations Have Been Understood as You Intended

a ripple effect on the daily routines. She wishes this information would be taken into consideration when decisions about schedules and special events are being made. To her, things like assemblies impact the natural rhythm of her time with students because they create varied levels of excitement for students, which forces the flow in the classroom to change in reaction to these emotions.

When students don't know what time they are getting out of class, or they are excited about an activity that will occur later, a carefully orchestrated lesson may have to be rushed and the teacher's tension rises figuring out how to manage it. Routines are important, and to deviate from them has an impact, especially when some students are not able to come back from the change in routine easily.

Paula is concerned with the number of pull-outs that happen with students when they are in her classroom. She doesn't think that administration has a clue about the number of times students are taken out of her class for reasons such as: discipline issues, to take medication, for an appointment outside of school, to talk with an administrator, to meet with a counselor, or various other things.

Paula has approximately forty minutes for a class that often includes hands-on activities. Guest speakers are also present in her room on a regular basis. She has asked her administrator for longer class periods, but until there is a change in the schedule, she doesn't see that happening. Additionally, she sees students less than the traditional school year calendar, so she only has a certain number of days to get her curriculum covered.

Ronald L. Partin has defined interruptions as what "is created when someone or some event causes you to stop an activity, at least temporarily" (Partin, 1987, p. 29). Classroom interruptions are those things that can cause a change in a schedule, no matter how miniscule. A phone call. A student being called to the office or another room. Announcements. A classroom visitor. Students joining the class late. Students leaving early. These are all things Ariel and Paula described as having happened in their class.

To highlight how often this can happen, Matthew Kraft and Manuel Monti-Nussbaum (2020) studied a school district in Rhode Island and found that classrooms were interrupted up to fifteen minutes per day (p. 31). Of the teachers they surveyed, 59 percent reported that the interruptions somewhat interfered with instruction. Using this data, the researchers found that three and a half minutes per hour are lost each school day. When a whole year was accounted for, they estimated that students lose between ten and twenty days of instruction time over the course of the school year due to interruptions.

While a minute or two of lost class time may not be detrimental to student learning on its own, the bigger issue is what the interruption does to the flow of a lesson. A daily lesson plan is a finely honed series of steps that are designed to create an experience where students develop a deeper understanding of a concept. Components of a lesson plan often include objectives, introductory activity, main lesson for students to complete, and follow up.

As in the case of Paula's classes, when there are only around forty minutes in a class, each minute is crucial. Depending upon when the interruption happens—beginning, middle, or end of class—students' attention is drawn away from the activity at hand. And in Ariel's case, the forty minutes is now thirty-eight minutes, which makes things even more difficult. And these changes have the potential to impact all students in the class.

Creating systems in which students know the procedures for things such as turning in work, starting class, or quieting down—and then practicing those moments—enhances a teacher's effectiveness. However, when the interruptions to class are unexpected or unable to be rehearsed, those are the moments that steal class time away from student learning. And these are the situations to which Ariel and Paula are referring. Interruptions to their class flow not only robs students of academic time, they also cause a rise in negative tension for both of them.

How does one alleviate the problem of interruptions? In 1986, the school board for the Fremont Unified School District in Fremont, California, developed Board Policy 6156.1 to deal with classroom interruptions. They required each school in their district to provide a plan to the board for review each year. With the goal being to limit the number of interruptions so students would have more instructional time, principals were directed to create and submit a plan to supervise and control activities that could impact the amount of instructional time. Brookvale's website (Brookvale, 1986) shows the plan included:

- Nonemergency announcements are all sent at the same time
- Classroom communication is limited to major emergencies
- Students check with the office at a specific time for items they had forgotten at home
- Students' being called to leave the classroom is lessened
- Students cannot be held over in one class, which would cause them to miss another class

Many of Paula's issues are addressed in this plan. These types of school-wide guidelines could create a system in which all stakeholders abide by and enforce the same policies. Are they too much? Perhaps not in a school where interruptions are high in number. These could be a recalibration to remind everyone that students should be in the classrooms as much as possible. There may be times that guidelines such as these cannot be followed, but perhaps those should be few and far between.

But what about Ariel's issues with completely altered schedules? How students respond to changes in Ariel's case could be related to classroom management techniques, like how a teacher manages the ebb and flow of a classroom. Robert Marzano, Barbara G. Gaddy, Maria Foseid, Mark Foseid, and Jana Marzano's book *A Handbook for Classroom Management That Works* (2005) states "Regardless of grade level, every teacher needs to deal with certain interruptions and transitions both within the classroom and from the classroom to other areas of the school or school grounds" (Marzano et al., 2005, p. 18). Their recommendations include:

- Setting rules and procedures for interruptions and transitions
- Practice how students should act during interruptions and transitions
- Giving students opportunities to take on leadership roles during these times

Even though there are unknown variables, setting up expectations ahead of time builds a foundation for both students and teachers to understand that even when changes occur unexpectedly, there are certain expectations that must still be maintained. Practicing these routines creates a pattern of action, and putting students in positions to take over some tasks such as passing out papers or answering the phone may help. Sometimes, though, this is easier said than done.

Teachers can be their own action researchers and collect data. Derrick Meador, a former educator and current superintendent of Jennings Public School in Oologah, Oklahoma, recommends keeping a journal for a period of time such as two weeks (Meador, 2019). At the end of collecting the data from the journal, it can be very beneficial to sift through the distractions and determine which ones can be dealt with and which ones need some sort of future action plan. Information such as this could help teachers like Ariel understand and prepare for those moments or days when negative tension is increasing and alleviate it.

Interruptions, no matter how insignificant they may seem, have the potential to steal learning time from students. There are policies that administrators can implement in their schools, but there are also small steps that teachers can take to reduce the overall impact on lost learning time. While Ariel's and Paula's tensions will continue to be possibilities, developing plans for when interruptions happen and then sharing those with students, modeling them, and practicing them may help reduce some of the time lost to interruptions that cannot be avoided.

PEOPLE: KNOW YOUR TEACHERS

Relationships between teacher and administrator was a strong theme that came up throughout all interviews. In situations where teachers felt they had a good relationship with administrators they were comfortable approaching them with any issues. Instances where the relationship was not as open or friendly actually caused an extra level of anxiety for the teachers.

Nicole had a dual role as both a teacher leader and a teacher, so she felt as if she could speak not only for herself, but her colleagues as well. JoAnne, additionally, felt her principal knew her and was working towards strengthening their relationship through academic-based discussions. And in her case, she was able to talk to her administrator using language that other teachers might not feel safe and secure using. Both teachers spoke glowingly of their administrators.

On the other hand, Delilah and Craig had instances where their relationships with the administrators were strained at best, and neither felt comfortable in approaching their principals about situations that were causing negative tension. This inability to voice concerns added to the negative tension they each were already feeling and actually caused it to build over time. Scenarios were created in which Delilah and Craig had physical reactions to their administrators.

The catch is that the relationship works two ways. Administrators have to be willing to be open with teachers and hear the good with the bad, and teachers have to be willing to be open with administrators, sharing both the good and the bad. Getting to know and trust individuals involves asking questions, making connections, and generally showing a sense of empathy and concern for people. But how does an administrator do that when they have so many teachers, support staff, students, and parents with whom to build relationships?

Craig and Delilah would say that this is where you must use your teachers' skills. Find what teachers are good at and put them in leadership roles, using their strengths to help keep a collective pulse on how the school is running. Let teachers lead in-services. Let teachers lead groups. Allow teachers to develop structures and activities that enhance the school setting for both adults and students.

How can administrators learn their staff members' strengths and skills? The answer is to get to know them. Grissom et al.'s 2021 report regarding the principal's effect on students and schools cited interacting with people as a necessary skill for administrators. Within this they found three components that impact the effectiveness of these interactions: caring, communication, and building trust (Grissom et al., 2021, p. 56). All three are connected and help build relationships. These three may seem like obvious ways to build relationships, but situations such as Delilah's and Craig's show that there is a need to understand why.

First, let's look at caring. Mark Smylie, Joseph Murphy, and Karen Seashore Louis (2016) define caring as "a quality of relationship, the matter, manner, and motivation of personal and professional action and interaction" (p. 6). Leaders set this as a priority in their settings, creating a culture of caring about others. Craig did not feel like he was cared about until another administrator stepped in and helped his situation.

And once Craig felt cared for, he was able to perpetuate that among his colleagues. He tapped into his empathic skills to not only coach and mentor his newest colleagues, but he was also able to help a new administrator navigate teacher observations. Creating a culture where caring about others is valued has the potential to ripple through a system in ways that are immeasurable.

A second skill successful principals utilize in relationship building is communication, according to the Grissom et al. (2021, p. 55). This again seems like an obvious response to creating relationships, but principals who created positive building cultures found purposeful communication to be a valuable tool. Research by Dr. Precious Kurth in 2016 found teachers expected their building leaders to be good communicators.

Engaging in purposeful communication includes a variety of methods to share information with staff. Open-door policies and being visible around the school and school grounds were found to be used effectively by principals (Grissom et al., 2021). Attending professional development sessions and engaging with staff in these types of settings gave administrators opportunities to communicate, share ideas, and understand the perspectives of their educators.

Dawn E. Tyler, EdD, looked at the communication behaviors of principals at high performing Title I elementary schools (2016). She found five themes of communication that were deemed important to the success the schools:

- Student-centered communication
- Trust
- Frequent communication
- Purposeful in-person communication
- Principals learned communication skills (Tyler, 2016, p. 7)

Roberta Salmirs Barber found teachers in a middle school preferred communication from an administrator via email over in-person discussion or meetings (Barber, 2020, p. 51). While we assume communication is necessary in any setting, understanding how these components are valued in a system can improve the relationships among school personnel, providing a path to sharing philosophies and perspectives in order to understand colleagues' beliefs and attempt to find a way to work together.

A final piece to the relationship puzzle is trust. Creating an environment of trust is a skill successful administrators utilize by earning the confidence of staff and knowing staff on a personal level (Hollingworth, Olsen, Asikin-Garmager, and Winn, 2017, pp. 9–13). How can administrators and teachers create an avenue where trust is present and valued? It is not an overnight process.

Jane Modoono, a former principal, says that trust is the most important factor in school. In her experiences, she says it takes at least three years to accomplish but is earned in every interaction during those small moments that do not involve teaching and learning: asking about family members or important moments in people's lives. Trust can then be in place during moments of stress or tension (Modoono, 2017).

Teachers also have a role in creating these relationships. They have the power to care, communicate, and build trust with colleagues and administrators; they do not have to wait for an administrator's blessing to do these things. And most teachers are doing this. But when negative tension has built up, and things look bleak or unwavering, an environment where caring, communication, and trust are present can help ease some of these tensions so teachers and administrators know their colleagues and who they can turn to.

Communication, trust, and caring are the foundation for relationships. Harnessing these interpersonal aspects of education help administrators and teachers alike get to know one another, and understand each other's perspectives, skills, and interests. Thus, when negative tensions arise and need to be dealt with, the players in the game already know each other and perhaps the relationship can sustain any stressful situations.

THE ORGANIZATION: KNOW YOUR EXPECTATIONS HAVE BEEN UNDERSTOOD AS YOU INTENDED

Teachers either consciously or subconsciously look towards their principals for guidance, so how an administrator organizes a system impacts how successful it will be in fulfilling the goals set forth. To do this, Fred C. Lunenberg (2010) lists three things that principals do at the building level to create the structure of the organization: developing the structure, hiring and training people, and putting in place methods to communicate necessary information. Of these three, our teachers had specific issues with communication or lack thereof.

Communication is a theme that runs through this section. The ability to communicate and the type of communication needed have previously been addressed. However, this section focuses on the outcomes of communication. How information is perceived by staff and how well it is followed were issues that caused negative tensions for our teachers. Communication includes a variety of methods such as face-to-face discussion, email, individual, and group.

Macy wanted her administrator to know that expectations are needed to manage student behaviors consistently among staff. She mentioned the word *expectation* twenty-one times during her interview. Macy puts a lot of pressure on herself but lacks confidence knowing where boundaries should be set; she wants her administrator to set these boundaries and then she expects everyone to follow them. This tension might only be Macy's, but she sees a lack of focus towards specific goals when expectations have not been laid out. She believed the staff could have a greater impact on student academics and behavior if there was consistent messaging.

Macy did acknowledge that there are different types of expectations, the known versus the unknown. The known expectations are ones that are specifically set; the unknown are those that teachers have to guess where the barometer is set. Macy referenced the frustration over these unknown expectations, saying teachers should know what is truly expected of them, and that expectation should be clearly communicated. Not having clear expectations leaves things ambiguous with no attainable goal.

How can these unknown expectations be reduced as a source of negative tension? Macy cited an instance where she was able to communicate her frustration with an administrator. The expectations for a circumstance were not clear, and the administrator admonished the entire staff for not following directions. This caused hurt feelings and created negative tension especially with those who had followed the rules.

A few days after the incident Macy approached her administrator and likened what had happened to a teacher punishing the whole class for the actions of a few students, saying, "You punished everyone instead of being clear about expectations." She felt empowered and justified in her action. Her administrator listened to her and took steps to rectify the situation with those who did not deserve the criticism.

While Macy wants her administrator to mark new lines in the sand, Jeff would love for his administrator to take the policies his school already has and communicate *what happened*. The lack of communication between what a particular administrator thinks or does versus what Jeff and his colleagues perceive to be occurring differ. Jeff cited an instance where a student's behavior was handled by administration, but Jeff was confused and underwhelmed by the consequences. He tried and failed to get an explanation for the result. Jeff said this left him with a sense that he should handle issues like this himself.

Both Macy and Jeff are looking for administrative expectations to be laid out, explained, and then followed. Are they asking for too much information? Would more information from administrators hamper a teacher's individuality in his or her own practice? Do all situations demand exact replication from administration and staff? Or is it acceptable to have guidelines but then have the flexibility to resolve each situation differently? Regardless, communication about the what and the why are important to these teachers.

What do our principals say about how to address these issues? Mitch noted that if a school is not aligned in how it views students and the role of education in students' lives, this is going to cause a lot of tension. The tension rests in the difference between what a school believes about students and what it believes about the purpose of school and its subsequent actions. If the two are not aligned then stakeholders are confused by the mixed messaging of words versus actions.

As a principal, Matt has good connections with his staff and they feel comfortable approaching him, giving him a pulse of what people are feeling, both positively and negatively. He has cultivated this by creating a friendly atmosphere and giving teachers the opportunity to lead things such as professional development. He has empowered his staff to help define the culture of his building and this has improved his ability to communicate with them.

When situations arise with his staff, Leo tries to take the emotion out in order to understand what is going on. In particular instances of student behavior, he looks to be a bridge between what students are doing and how teachers are responding in order to find a solution rather than creating a definitive rule that everyone must follow. He was purposeful in listening to both sides with students and teachers to earn their trust when handling precarious situations.

Antony referenced the fact that sometimes when a teacher sends a student to his office, five hundred other things are happening at the same time, so he takes care of the student issue and moves on to the next fire. As a result, communication with the teacher is not always there and he knows this frustrates teachers. But, he also noted that the teacher needs to have the initiative to come back and ask what happened; communication needs to be a two-way street.

Teachers like Macy and Jeff and all of our other educators take their roles seriously. If given parameters, they will develop a way to succeed. Without an understanding of the what and why of a situation they feel left out and negative tensions seem to increase. Should other teachers not understand the expectations, then a consistent pattern cannot be followed for all scenarios. Our teachers want their administrators to know that.

HOW TEACHERS CAN COMMUNICATE
THESE TOPICS WITH ADMINISTRATORS

Caralee Adams in her article "How to Ask Your Principal for Anything" (2012) recommends four things for teachers to consider when approaching their administrator.

1. A teacher should have a plan that includes knowing the administrator being asked and understanding how the question or topic fits into the overall school goals.
2. Know when the best time to ask is. This involves determining when an administrator is going to be open to the question.
3. How should you ask? Email? Face-to-face conversation? Personalized note? This will depend on a teacher's comfort level with both the administrator and the topic.
4. Know specifically what you are asking for and how you envision it being accomplished. And finally, be confident. (Adams, 2012)

These steps are manageable for some issues, but there are those topics that Roland Barth (2002) calls *nondiscussables*. These are the topics that lead to negative tension, the things that cannot be talked about in the open for fear of the consequences. These are the topics that the teachers described with the deepest sense of frustration, the things that can exacerbate negative tensions.

All of the teachers indicated nondiscussables either because of the topic itself or because of the outcome of discussing it. Jeff felt there were things he could not talk about with his team because he did not know how it would impact their overall relationships. JoAnne had to limit what she shared with her team regarding her conversations with her principal. Delilah valued her administrator's view of her as an educator and did everything she could to not rock the boat.

The lower the number of nondiscussables in a school, the healthier the school is. Barth points to school leaders as the ones who are responsible for naming these topics and getting them out in the open (Barth, 2002). But how does an administrator or even a teacher leader approach topics that could cause strife in the working relationship? It turns out, other industries have nondiscussables as well and have confronted these issues.

It helps to look outside of education where nondiscussables are already part of the lexicon. Ginka Toegel and Jean-Louis Barsoux (2016) work with companies and say that nondiscussables exist because people are afraid of the repercussions if they are brought out into the open. Teams don't want to broach these topics because they feel team collegiality will be upset, when in fact the opposite is true. Toegel and Barsoux have actually found that people feel unburdened when these topics are discussed; there is relief and the sense of team increases. There is value in a team facing the fire together.

There are layers of nondiscussables. Power balances, people saying things they do not feel, unnamed feelings, and unconscious actions by some are situations that lead to topics being taboo. What are strategies for discussing these? Toegel and Barsoux suggest not making immediate judgments. Hear people out, analyze progress towards goals, see the perspectives of others, and in extreme cases, invite a third party in to observe and report on interactions between group members in meetings (Toegel and Barsoux, 2016).

The point of writing all of these nondiscussables here is not to say that principals and other administrators need to explicitly follow these suggestions. They are intended to be a source of understanding for all stakeholders in education that ugly, negative tensions do exist. And, when they arise or grow, there are lenses through which to look at them before deciding on a definitive solution.

Teachers like Nicole and JoAnne are in ideal situations where they already have good relationships with their administrators in which they feel supported and valued. However, not all of our teachers feel that way. So what does all of this mean? It means that the system, colleagues, expectations, and communication—four of the seven themes in this book—do matter. It means that deliberate actions can increase the relationships that need to exist for these tensions to be addressed. It means that a system of colleagues needs to have consistent expectations and a culture where discussion of the positives and negatives of them is welcomed.

REFLECTIVE QUESTIONS

1. How is student time in class viewed in your setting?
2. How well do you feel you know your colleagues?
3. How well are expectations followed in your setting?
4. What are your strengths in building relationships with your colleagues? What areas are weaknesses for you?
5. What does communication look like in your setting?

REFERENCES

Adams, Caralee. (2012). "How to Ask Your Principal for Anything." Scholastic. Scholastic Teacher. https://www.scholastic.com/teachers/articles/teaching-content/how-ask-your-principal-anything/.

Barber, Roberta Salmirs. (2020). "A Case Study of Communications between School Administrators and Teachers in an Urban Middle School," EdD diss., Indiana University.

Barth, Roland S. (2002). "The Culture Builder." *Educational Leadership* 59(8): 6–11.

Brookvale Elementary School. (1986). "Classroom Interruptions." Fremont Unified School District. https://brookvale-fusd-ca.schoolloop.com/pf4/cms2/view_page?d=x&group_id=1548492092439&vdid=6i18e2t63pq723f.

Grissom, Jason, Anna Egalite, and Constance Lindsay. (2021). "How Principals Affect Students and Schools: A Systematic Synthesis of Two Decades of Research." Wallace Foundation. https://www.wallacefoundation.org/knowledge-center/pages/how-principals-affect-students-and-schools-a-systematic-synthesis-of-two-decades-of-research.aspx.

Hollingworth, Liz, Dorian Olsen, Asih Asikin-Garmager, and Kathleen M. Winn. (2017). "Initiating Conversations and Opening Doors." *Educational Management Administration & Leadership* 46(6): 1014–1034. https://doi.org/10.1177/1741143217720461.

Institute of Education Sciences. (2019). "Digest of Education Statistics, 2019." National Center for Education Statistics (NCES) Home Page, a part of the U.S. Department of Education. Accessed May 9, 2021. https://nces.ed.gov/programs/digest/d19/tables/dt19_209.10.asp?current=yes.

Kraft, Matthew, and Manuel Monti-Nussbaum. (2020). "The Big Problem with Little Interruptions to Classroom Learning." (EdWorkingPaper: 20–227). Retrieved from Annenberg Institute at Brown University. https://doi.org/10.26300/6b7g-nm11.

Lunenburg, Fred C. (2010). "The Principal and the School: What Do Principals Do?" *National Forum of Education Administration and Supervision Journal* 27(4): 1–13.

Marzano, Robert J. et al. (2005). *A Handbook for Classroom Management that Works*. ASCD.

Meador, Derrick. (2019). "Strategies for Teachers to Maximize Student Learning Time." ThoughtCo. DotDash, June 24, 2019. https://www.thoughtco.com/strategies-for-teachers-to-maximize-student-learning-time-4065667.

Modoono, Jane. (2017). "The Trust Factor." *Educational Leadership* 74(8).

Partin, Ronald L. (1987). "Minimizing Classroom Interruptions." *The Clearing House: A Journal of Educational Strategies, Issues and Ideas* 61(1): 29–31. https://doi.org/10.1080/00098655.1987.10113905.

Smylie, Mark A., Joseph Murphy, and Karen Seashore Louis. (2016). "Caring School Leadership: A MultiDisciplinary, Cross-Occupational Model." *American Journal of Education* 123(1): 1–35. https://doi.org/10.1086/688166.

Toegel, Ginka, and Jean-Louis Barsoux. (2016). "How to Preempt Team Conflict." *Harvard Business Review*. https://hbr.org/2016/06/how-to-preempt-team-conflict.

Tyler, Dawn E. (2016). "Communication Behaviors of Principals at High Performing Title I Elementary Schools in Virginia: School Leaders, Communication, and Transformative Efforts." *Creighton Journal of Interdisciplinary Leadership* 2(2): 2–16. https://doi.org/10.17062/cjil.v2i2.51.

Chapter 5

What We Wish Teachers Knew

Within any organization there can be an underlying tension that the managers, supervisors, principals, or superintendents simply do not have a clear picture of the daily responsibilities and pressure of their subordinates. In some cases, the tension can result in frayed relationships, low morale, and in extreme situations toxic culture. For a leader, the same tension can grow within them, when the people they lead do not understand, or know, what their leader does to support their people. When this disconnect happens it can leave everyone feeling lost, frustrated, and wishful.

In many situations, a principal may receive a directive from the district office, or even the school board, to implement a new policy or procedure. The policy may be something the principal does not personally support, but their responsibility is to carry out the directives of their superiors with fidelity and without impudence.

The principal may receive support or questions from their staff about the policy or initiative. In either case, the principal is unable to share the discussions that may or may not have happened prior to the decision being made. Not being able to share important discussions can leave some staff members questioning if they can rely on support from their principal. This is what Antony wishes his teachers knew: how much he fights for them.

> I wish sometimes they knew how much we fought for them. I know when it's a decision that they don't like I'm usually in agreement with the teachers. I may not like the decision either, but the decision has been made and now I—we—have to support the decision. I wish they knew that, man, there were a lot of bruises and fighting and sweating that went into the decision. Sometimes what we want doesn't happen. That doesn't mean I'm not going to step out of the batter's box and stop swinging. I'll keep swinging for them as long as I can. I just feel bad that my batting average is so low.

The quote from Antony might leave the impression that the job of a principal is mired in tension that involves a perpetual scoreboard that tallies wins and losses. That is not the case. It is true that within all organizations there are battles over philosophy, mission, and accountability. As organizations, schools are no different. Teachers and leaders are passionate advocates for children and sometimes the passion can bubble into tensions. For teachers, it can be hard to understand all of the debates, conversations, and passionate exchanges that are happening between administrators as they make decisions that affect students and teachers.

Teachers are busy taking care of their students, while administrators are busy taking care of their teachers. It is not unlike a teacher who advocates for her students with the principal. Sometimes they get what they ask for and sometimes they do not. When that happens, the teachers can not return to the classrooms and discredit the principal, even when it would be easier to let the students know the teacher tried their best, but did not get what they were hoping for from the conversation.

In some cases, tension can grow as a result of individuals in the organization not completely understanding the roles and responsibilities of our colleagues. It is hard to describe all the duties an aide, office manager, custodian, teacher, or administrator has throughout the day. When tensions begin to run high in a building it is easier to begin to question what the principal really does during the day. There is a saying that goes something like this, "On some days we get paid too much, and others we don't get paid enough."

On the days in which everything is flowing as it should, getting paid too much may look like not working hard enough to the people in the building who feel like they are not getting paid enough on that day. Because the daily schedule of a principal may be less prescribed than a classroom teacher's schedule, this can cause tension between the principal and the teacher.

While principals may not have a prescribed daily schedule, that does not mean their schedules are empty. Usually filled with meetings, classroom observations, or phone calls to parents, the principal's day often consists of work that is invisible to teachers. While the principal looks to be on the phone, those phone calls can be tense, and may be buffering teachers from other issues.

> I don't think they understand, I would love for them to walk in my shoes for a day. Just to see the things that go on a daily basis. They (teachers) have no idea of some of the phone calls I might get from a parent. Or when I change my schedule to cover a classroom or supervision because someone needs to leave early.

Knowing that he adjusts his schedule to support his teachers, Matt believes many of his teachers know that he shields the teachers from parent phone calls. Knowing that his teachers recognize he supports them does help to minimize some of the tension, but on some days, he says, "When I have done things to help out and someone complains about how I handled something with a parent can make me want to react. I don't react, but inside it hurts."

Matt chooses not to react when he feels hurt inside. What would happen if he did react? By reacting he can resolve the tension before it becomes overwhelming and a threat to the school culture. Reacting to the hurt he is feeling does not mean he needs to react with anger or frustration. Instead, communicating with his teacher how he spoke with a parent about the situation strengthened Matt's bond of communication with the teacher, which builds a culture of trust and open communication.

It also helps the teacher understand what Matt did during the day. To help teachers understand what principals and other building leaders do, the building leaders must be willing to have conversations and share their experiences. When we share with others what we do, it resolves misperceptions about the situation. Everyone learns and grows together while strengthening the culture.

Leo's tension related to what he wished teachers knew about his job also relates to shielding teachers from parents. In addition, Leo experiences a high level of tension by shouldering many of the student discipline issues.

> I probably overprotect them (the teachers) from parents. I take on a lot of parent stuff that they don't see. I make a lot of phone calls that should be coming from the classroom teacher but I end up taking some of those phone calls so I can clear the teachers' plates. One of my strengths is my ability to connect with parents and I think that comes from having a lot of hard conversations about mental health when I was a school counselor. I probably should do a better job of coaching the teachers on how to have hard conversations with parents. But I'm also not sure about that (teachers having hard conversations with parents).
>
> When I'm talking to a parent about a kid being suicidal and how they are on the verge of wanting to kill themselves, I'm not sure a teacher should have that conversation. I have a background as a counselor. That's what I did before being a principal. In those situations I take the brunt of those calls and that creates stress for me. Because of the nature of the call, I can share some things, but sometimes I keep some of that information confidential.
>
> That caused tension between me and some of the teachers. They feel they need to know and I don't feel the same. I just wish they would trust that I handled the situation. Most of the teachers do trust that I handled the situation. It's the two or three that don't that can really make me question my approach.

Wishing all of the teachers trusted him to handle the situation creates tension for Leo. While he is comfortable having hard conversations with parents, he seems to struggle to have hard conversations with some of his teachers.

If he had those hard conversations, perhaps wishing for trust may transform to actual trust.

The implementation of new curriculum resources, school-wide behavior plans, scheduling changes, or systemic changes is one of the major responsibilities of the principal. In some cases, there may be staff members that have been through their fair share of changes within their school. If staff have experienced a good amount of change or new initiatives while in their school it can leave them feeling exhausted. Instead of strengthening their skills and becoming exceptional in an area, it feels that—just when they are starting to get things working efficiently—the system changes again. This creates tension for both teachers and administrators.

Changes and initiatives are not often considered without a great deal of planning. Mitch is a high school principal who is working to bring some needed change to his school. While he believes the change is needed, the process has left him feeling inadequate. He wished his teachers knew how much time and planning had gone into the change and that they would consider that before casting judgment.

> I feel like a lot of time there's planning that's going on that hasn't necessarily been made public. The planning will eventually be shared, but it's just not totally there yet. When you have a staff of seventy individuals some of them are on one end of the spectrum with their planning where they wanted this information two weeks ago. Because you didn't give them the information when they asked for it, you are left feeling inadequate. It feels like they are saying you have not even thought of this. You are not organized. You are not doing the things I need to feel supported.

When Mitch hears those things he says he can become a bit defensive. While the planning team has not considered everything, they have planned for many issues. "People are questioning whether you have thought through everything and sometimes you get defensive yourself. I want to say just relax. We're working through stuff, but we aren't ready to get this information to you yet, but we will take care of you. Just understand that we are doing our due diligence to make sure we are making an informed decision." In all the situations that were explored, every principal did not let their staff know these feelings were causing them tension.

Wishing that teachers knew the extent to which principals planned before they made a decision also resonated with Matt.

> I wish teachers knew the time that goes into the planning to roll out initiatives. I spend a lot of time looking at the data to support my decisions. They don't see any of that stuff. I think there's a lot more than people are aware of. And it's not

something I share, it's just you know, you just do it because it's best for kids and that is my focus, the kids.

Matt's focus is on the needs of his students. That is the same focus for his teachers and yet it does not seem that either Matt or his teachers are sharing this perspective with one another. Instead, the planning and reviewing of data is done within a silo that perpetuates a silent tension. When these tensions exist because of a lack of open communication, this becomes a threat to the culture of the school.

Other principals wished their teachers knew the thought and effort they devoted to helping them grow as professionals. Leo is an assistant principal with a background in counseling. He has never been a classroom teacher. The lack of experience as a classroom teacher sometimes results in tension between him and his teachers. When he provides feedback to them regarding their teaching he can be met with: "You don't know what it's like to be in a classroom."

While it is true he has never been a classroom teacher, it does not mean his feedback should be dismissed. He recognizes this is a challenge for him and he is working to build relationships with his teachers in order to facilitate a collaborative atmosphere.

> Well I guess I try to build that relationship with teachers to showcase that we're doing this together. Then I use what I see in other classrooms to have a coaching conversation with another teacher who may be struggling. I let them know that I was just in this teacher's classroom and they tried this, why don't you go connect with Mary about this thing that happened in the classroom.

As Leo attempts to build relationships with his teachers and build a collaborative culture, he feels the tension when teachers feel he is comparing one against the other. "I believe at the end of the day they're not going to learn stuff from me. They're going to learn stuff from the other teachers. My job is to create experiences where they can communicate with each other and build on the expertise that's in the room next to them."

Leo is trying to show his teachers the expertise they collectively share. He also feels that the tension builds because his teachers continue to push him and remind him he has never been in the classroom. He does not need to be reminded of that fact; he is well aware he has not been a teacher. Leo also believes it is his job to help the teachers he works with to grow and learn even if he has never taught in a classroom. "I've never taught in a classroom longer than a day. I've only ever done single lessons. But I've been in enough classrooms to know what students experience and what helps them learn."

All of the principals also wished the teachers they worked with understood what they went through when disciplining students. The principals all agreed that tension grows when teachers perceive they (the principals) have not delivered what they perceive to be the appropriate consequence for the behavior in question. Additionally, they recognize that they could improve on the manner in which they communicate the result of the student's visit to the office. For Leo, discipline was rife with tension.

> I was still so focused on school counseling that I don't think I was as effective as I could have been. Figuring out how to discipline, that was really a big tension . . . that was a hard learning curve for me. I had such internal conflict with myself, but then when I would try to go help teachers with disruptive students (then it's) you don't know what it's like to be a teacher. So my approach wasn't even valued or validated. Like anything that I said didn't matter because I didn't have classroom experience.

The tension grew because the teachers Leo was working with did not seem to value his background experience working with students. He wished that they had more respect for what he knew and what he could offer to help the student and teacher create a better environment. He knew he had to make a change and had to build relationships with the teachers with whom he worked.

> My focus last year was listening, building relationships, and building people's strengths. I would listen and I nodded my head, and really built relationships so that people could trust me. So now I feel a little bit more comfortable speaking my truth because now they can trust me even if I don't have classroom experience.

WHAT TENSIONS PRINCIPALS FILTER

One of the assumptions made when we work with others is that they do not know what the responsibilities of other people in the organization are. This is the case for the principals, from the previous section of this chapter. They assume the teachers with whom they work do not understand or recognize the planning, the thoughtfulness with student discipline, or the amount of parent issues they, as principals, buffer for their staff. However, when teachers are asked what tensions do your principals filter for you, they seemingly have a good grasp of what their principals are doing behind the scenes during the school day.

Nicole understands what tensions her principals filter for her. When one of the principals in her building spends the time to filter things so that she does not have to devote time to the issue, she is afforded the time and energy to focus on the needs of her students. One of the tensions that Nicole appreciates her principal addressing is working with parents. She recognizes there are expectations she must first do before reaching out to her principal, but once it is in the hands of the principal, she can focus on her students.

> Definitely parents. And I'll put a little caveat on that; I think our administration in our building expects that we deal with it as best we can. When it seems like we're not making progress we loop them in on the situation. I generally found that they respect the fact that we're not just tossing things to them. "I have a problem with this kid or this parent—you deal with it."

> But if I document these are the things I've done and I haven't been making much progress or we're going backwards, they will step in to support me. I feel like at some point when they step in, they filter the conversations and communication from me . . . I've found multiple situations where they've told the parent we're done and this conversation is over. They sort of take it off your plate.

In this situation, Nicole may not be aware of how many phone calls, email exchanges, or meetings between the principal and the parent have happened, but she recognizes they are happening. Because the principal filters the more difficult situations, she is able to reduce her own tension.

Macy, an elementary teacher, concurred with Nicole that the principal in her building filtered tensions that may be the result of parental concerns.

> If anything, I'd say maybe certain parents. Some parents need more attention. Sometimes more attention than I can give. He will take the time to meet with them and talk with them. He tells me when he is meeting with them, and I'm sure he filters what has been said so he doesn't get me upset. Which can make me upset, I want to know what they said. I think he will also decide when he needs to tell them (parents) how it's going to be and not let them kind of take over the situation so much.

Macy mentioned that when her principal filters what parents say in meetings from her, it can be frustrating. However, she has come to realize there is a reason for her principal's approach to the situation.

> He has told me that he believes if the parent is going to be frustrated with someone it should be him. He wants me and the parent to have a positive relationship so we can do what is best for the student. He does not want the parents to be frustrated with me.

In this situation the tension continues to exist, but Macy realizes her principal is doing what he can to support her, her student, and the parents.

Recognizing the amount of time and effort put into the planning and implementation of policy or instructional changes was one topic principals wished that teachers understood better. Macy, an elementary teacher, recognized the time required of principals to prepare for a new initiative. In addition, she could understand when her principal did not share details about the planning.

> He won't share details for anything he doesn't know for sure. I think he doesn't want us to worry about things that are still in the planning stages. He knows we are all pretty Type A. He reminds us to hold off on certain things until he knows more. I don't think he's going to be like, yeah we're thinking about doing this when it's in the first stages. I think he tried to be careful about that—getting us too excited about things.

Preventing the staff from getting "too excited" about things helps to reduce tensions for the teachers. Macy understands the purpose of not sharing information and she understands the amount of time that is devoted to planning. She understands these things because she also has a line of communication to her principal.

Ariel, a middle school teacher, appreciates when her principal supports her and her students when behavior needs to be addressed.

> I feel like all administrators I've had tend to take on the really disruptive students and work with them and their parents and we just see the surface. I don't think we always see the depth of that time. So sometimes I think as teachers we don't appreciate that our administrators take the lead on that for us. I think for better or worse things with parents are filtered. I feel like there have been times in my past when parents have gone directly to administrators and if it's something that I can fix my administrator has come to me. If it's something that I can't fix, my administrator will find the support to help me and the student.

Ariel is in a unique position in her building. She is an identified teacher leader. Because she also has a role as a teacher leader in the building, she is part of conversations with her principal in which she knows explicitly what her principal filters from her and her colleagues. She and her principal have conversations about planning, parent phone calls, discipline, and the tensions her principal is experiencing. Because of that she is able to be an advocate when other teachers begin to question "what the principal really does."

THE WISDOM OF A GRANDMOTHER

A wise grandmother once said, "You can crap in one hand and wish in the other, and see which one fills up first." There are many things that teachers wished principals knew about their jobs. Likewise, principals wish teachers knew the many things about their jobs that create tension. Wishing rarely results in significant change or relieves underlying tension. In fact, wishing does little to leverage the positive power of tensions. Teachers recognize that their principals filter many tensions.

The tensions that principals feel when they wish their teachers knew what they filtered from them is the result of teachers not knowing what is being filtered. As Brené Brown (2018) has stated: "Clarity is Kind." When principals filter too much, they run the risk of being isolated and feeling that no one understands what they are going through.

Being an educator at any level is hard. There is continual change as well as constant bombardment from societal forces. Left unchecked, the bombardment from outside forces can seep into the schoolhouse. The forces that seep in can permeate a school and pose a threat to the culture and the climate of the school. The principal is the gatekeeper. It is their filtering that will determine what tensions the teachers and staff in the building will experience. When the principal is left with this task it is exhausting.

Depending on how the principal responds can determine whether or not she feels isolated in her work or supported in her work in filtering tensions. What we have learned from the experiences of the principals and teachers in this chapter is that when there is a disconnect in communication, principals are not only left wishing what their teachers knew, but they experience tension as a result.

Strong communication within a school organization can have a positive impact on establishing a positive school culture. When communication is inconsistent, or fractured, the resulting school culture becomes less strong and less positive. While Antony, Mitch, Leo, and Matt all believed they had fostered a strong communication pipeline between them and their teachers, the communication link omitted sharing the behind-the-scenes work that they did on a daily basis.

That omission left them wishing their teachers knew how much they fought for them, how much they planned, and how much they protected their teachers from disruptions in their school day whether it was from parents, students, or other colleagues. The tension they experienced was the result of an internal battle. What information can I share? What information cannot be shared? With whom can I share information?

These questions seemed to be reserved for beginning principals. However, Antony, Mitch, and Matt all are experienced administrators and yet they all wish their teachers knew what they did to protect the teachers from tensions. The tensions they are experiencing are not reserved for new administrators. These tensions can be experienced by all administrators.

The next step for a principal who is wishing that their staff knew what they did behind the scenes is to recognize that most of the staff does recognize what administrators do behind the scenes. Additionally, most teachers are grateful for the work administrators do behind the scenes. What both teachers and administrators can do is to acknowledge the tension and leverage it for change.

In Jennifer Abrams's book *Having Hard Conversations* (2009), she identifies a number of steps to facilitate having hard conversations:

- Identify why they hesitate having hard conversations
- Choose questions to ask themselves before they choose to speak up
- Articulate in professional language the challenges they are facing
- Determine the goals of the conversation and write an action plan of support
- Script the conversation avoiding trigger words that put others on the defensive
- Choose the best "wheres" and "whens" for a productive discussion

It may seem strange that principals would need a reminder of how to have a hard conversation. Being a leader, it can be assumed that hard conversations are part of the role. However, many administrators, teachers, parents, and the general public avoid hard conversations. For principals, having a hard conversation with their teachers about what the responsibilities entail for a principal may seem self-serving. Principals are supposed to serve others. When principals ask for—what can be perceived as—acknowledgment for their service, it can be uncomfortable.

The first step in having a hard conversation is to identify why it is hard to have that conversation. As many of the principals noted, they do not often react when teachers do not recognize the work they have done to help cover a classroom or to manage tension-filled situations with a parent or student. But they do feel hurt. When they feel hurt, they internalize the tension and it slowly grows and builds. It is uncomfortable and harmful if left unchecked. It can impact the interaction with teachers, staff, or students.

Having a conversation about feeling hurt can be challenging. In order to maintain a strong culture, principals need to model what they want from their teachers. Sharing how they feel—minimized and unrecognized for their efforts—makes them hurt and defeated. When they show their vulnerability they give permission to others to do the same. A culture that is built on communication and care will build a strong foundation for success.

Being vulnerable to share what principals wished their staff knew about their roles and responsibilities is not an impulsive decision. To have the conversation the principal needs to consider how to have the conversation.

They should consider the information they want to share and the questions they want to ask, taking great care that the conversation is not accusatory or threatening in tone.

When a principal has a hard conversation with a staff member, the principal should recognize the power differential between the two people having the conversation. The purpose of the conversation should be to share information in order to relieve the tension and to model that dialogue. Conversations to minimize this tension is to help others understand, not to force them to understand.

When the tensions principals experience, and the corresponding wish about what they wish teachers knew, are manifested in feelings, having a hard conversation could be treacherous. Feeling hurt, dismissed, or minimized affects everyone. Principals and teachers work hard and devote their lives to serving others. It can be devastating to experience tensions and feelings that threaten that work. When harnessing tensions to have a hard conversation, language is important.

Using language that is laced with emotion and accusation can undermine the intent of the meeting, increase tension, and challenge the culture of the school. Instead, language needs to be planned and carefully considered. Again, the intent of having a conversation is to build a culture in which the foundation is communication and relationships.

Language during this meeting cannot be undervalued. Taking the time to consider the origins of the tension and the impact on the individual is critical to determine the script and purpose of the meeting. Scripting and planning the conversation does not reduce the authenticity of the conversation. It may, in fact, enhance the authenticity.

When people take time to consider their thoughts, not only from their view but the view of the person they are having the conversation with, they show care and concern for the other person. When we choose to react to our tensions with impulsivity we are driven by emotion. Antony has had those experiences when he has allowed his emotions to get the best of him. When he has responded impulsively and with emotion the fallout can take a long time to correct.

> I'm an emotional person. I made so many mistakes, and still do, when I don't control my emotions. I've learned over time that I can still be passionate without being emotional. When my emotion outweighs my passion, I find people stop listening. They don't hear the passion or what I'm saying. Instead they feel like, I better not piss him off because he gets mad. Thankfully, I had a few people who told me to knock it off. I listened to them and I think we are all better off.

If a staff member is fearful of "pissing someone off," they will not be comfortable in having hard and important conversations. If that happens the communication, trust, and relationship culture of the school will be threatened.

Timing is everything. Unfortunately, tensions do not follow time or any other schedule. Tensions are always present and will always be part of our work. To leverage tensions, it is important when it may be most effective to have a hard conversation about tensions. In Daniel Pink's book *When: The Scientific Secrets of Perfect Timing* (2018), he explains when is the best time in the day to make decisions, and to have hard conversations.

In Pink's research, he has found that people feel more warm and engaged with others in the morning. During the afternoon, people feel less warm towards others. In the evening, our feelings toward others begin to rebound and we feel greater warmth. Knowing this information, it is important for principals who want to address tensions to consider sharing the information in the morning or later in the day. Having a mid-afternoon conversation may result in a negative experience.

Using the advice of a wise grandmother who reminded us that "we can wish in one hand and crap in the other and see which one fills up first," we need to move away from wishing and adopt a mindset of doing. As we have learned from the principals and the teachers in this chapter they experience tension when there is a breakdown in communication.

To build a viable culture that is built on communication, trust, and relationships we must be willing to leverage the tension we feel to impact change. Simply wishing our teachers knew things about what principals do is a waste of time and energy. We do not wish our students learned how to read, wish they performed better on an assessment, or wish they behaved better. We take action.

Addressing tension requires us to be comfortable with the uncomfortable. This means as leaders, we must be willing to be vulnerable. When we are vulnerable and willing to show the desire to have an authentic, clear, hard conversation we grow in our trust of one another. Trust between a principal and the teachers allows for the little tensions to dissolve so that there can be more focus on the big tensions.

REFLECTIVE QUESTIONS

1. What are the things you wished your teachers knew? Why do they not know them? What will you do to share those things with your teachers?
2. What is preventing you from being vulnerable with your staff? Is being vulnerable important to the culture in your school?

3. How have you leveraged the personal tensions you feel to make positive changes within your school?

REFERENCES

Abrams, Jennifer. (2009). *Having Hard Conversations*. Corwin.
Brown, Brené. (2018). *Daring to Lead: Brave Work, Tough Conversations, Whole Hearts*. Random House.
Pink, Daniel. (2018). *When: The Scientific Secrets of Perfect Timing*. Riverhead Books.

Chapter 6

How Do We Take Care of Each Other?

Craig's experiences demonstrate how a negative system, lack of expectations, and isolation among colleagues can devastate even the most confident of teachers. Craig immediately felt out of place in his new position. He didn't know anything about the program he was creating, and instead of getting help from his administrator, Craig was asked to do things he was not comfortable with. Things became so tense that when he would see this administrator in the hallway, she would turn away from him and Craig would feel his hands shake as anger and frustration welled up inside of him in these instances, impacting his health and well-being.

The lack of relationships with his colleagues impacted Craig in a negative manner as well. In his first staff meeting at his new school, as he sat down and began to introduce himself to a new colleague, she got up and walked away. He felt many colleagues judged him harshly thinking this was simply an easy teaching position he was taking before retirement. The negative tension he felt caused him to lose his self-confidence and self-assuredness. He says he "forgot who he was." His personal health suffered as did his teaching practice.

THE ISSUE

There is power in having a group of people to confer with when struggles and negative tension arise. To keep oneself from becoming isolated during difficult times it is imperative for teachers and administrators to find their people, the ones who can relate to the issues being faced. However, there is a distinct difference between having a go-to group that simply complains and vents, versus a group that problem solves and grows together. The latter has the potential to turn the negative tensions into positive growth, while the former tends to perpetuate negative feelings.

A group that has a common vision and goals along with the belief that they can successfully accomplish the tasks before them is said to have collective efficacy. This construct was introduced by Albert Bandura in the 1990s following his research regarding self-efficacy of individuals. His research on self-efficacy showed that when people perceive that they are able to complete a desired task, this belief affects the outcome of that task (Bandura, 1998, p. 53).

Bandura added that since people do not live their lives as "isolates" they work with others to produce results: "People's shared beliefs in their collective power to produce desired outcomes is a crucial ingredient of collective agency. Group performance is the product of interactive and coordinative dynamics of its members" (Bandura, 1998, p. 53). In other words, individual performances have an impact on the entire group.

Researcher John Hattie, in 2019, put collective teacher efficacy as the number one factor affecting student achievement in his list of performance indicators. When teachers believe they can make a difference they believe they impact learning (Hattie, 2019). Schools where collective teacher efficacy (CTE) is higher have greater expectations for student success and teachers have a vested interest in the success of students that school as a whole.

Components of CTE, according to author Jenni Donohoo (2016), include:

- The amount of teacher leadership present
- Clear building goals
- Responsive leaders who show concern for their staff

The teachers interviewed echo these components as being important to deal with negative tensions, but they also added one more component: a sense of collegiality. Together, these components helped to keep tensions at bay. How does a school build this sense of collective teacher efficacy, and how can teachers build their own efficacious groups in order to help tension levels?

As a teacher, one has a decision to make about how much collegiality is important. At times it may feel easier for a teacher to step into his or her classroom, close the door, and deal with all situations that arise alone. To not display any perceived weaknesses. To not ask for help or guidance. It is ironic, really, that adults ask students to have a growth mindset and yet it is difficult for some adults to give up the facade of perfection.

Within teaching there are so many variables to be controlled. Teachers expressed the belief that they are professionals and should be able to solve the problems they face. However, in reality, if a building has a set vision then it falls to everyone in said building to work towards those goals, not just one solitary teacher. A school will not succeed if everyone is not vested in the system's vision. The next sections explore the constructs of collegiality, teacher leadership, clear building goals, and responsive leaders with teachers and administrators.

COLLEGIALITY

When tensions arise, all teachers and administrators here talked about having a tribe or a close group of people to relate to. In the teachers' cases, it was usually grade level or content-area colleagues, people whom our subjects saw on a regular basis and shared similar experiences. Nicole talked about how important lunch was for her content-area group to grow as a team.

Paula, a teacher who feels isolated by her content and her space in the school, spoke of the excitement when an in-service day brought the whole staff together. She was able to talk to people she had not seen since the school year began. However, in such a safe space, Nicole cautioned that it is important for the issues to either be dropped or for solutions to be found. Dwelling on issues, in her situation, tended to sustain the negative tension, whereas when the group worked to solve a problem tensions could somewhat be alleviated.

Staff lounges often get a reputation for being dens of negativity where all teachers do is talk about the negative aspects of the job. And that can happen. The reality is, though, that tension is present and at times needs to be vented. But to simply talk about negative topics loses a valuable opportunity for frank discussions. What if one teacher in that lounge listened and then asked, "Well, what should we do about it?" Could that change the lens of how tension is looked at and then handled by that group? Would this, as in Nicole's situation, help alleviate negative tension and turn it into a positive outcome?

If these discussions occur, it is then important for administrators to accept the results of these group conversations as viable solutions. Informal discussions, without set agendas, are open, honest, and viable opportunities for problem solving as much as formal meetings. If teachers were to approach an administrator with lunchtime talk solutions, even if they are not able to be implemented, administrators should accept them as important teacher input.

Finding colleagues to confer with is an important component that could be a challenge. What could have helped Craig in his situation? Teachers here talked about finding their tribes of like-minded people in a variety of ways. Craig discussed a previous experience being at an international conference and after assigning himself to a lunch table, found himself seated at a table with fellow teachers from his state. He believes people with similarities naturally gravitate towards each other; he has trust in the fact that he will naturally find his tribe.

In his final years of teaching, Craig did find those people who had the same vision as he. He ultimately finished his career with a strong group of colleagues who supported him and whom he was able to support using his mentoring skills. It was the culture that a new administrator built that supported an environment where working together was valued. Craig once again felt like he was a strong teacher.

Ariel, with twenty-three years of experience, recommended listening to what colleagues say in staff meetings and watching what groups people are part of both in and out of school. She makes sure to connect in some way, via email or visiting the teacher's classroom, to discuss the similar interests. Ariel feels this gives her a variety of people to go to beyond those in her grade level or subject area.

Delilah and Macy both value people who tell them the truth about scenarios, and even though they sometimes are not ready to hear the message being given, they count these as colleagues to go to when negative tension arises. Both referenced finding people who can wade through the emotion of the tension to help clarify the situation. Each felt a high level of comfort with the people they put in these roles. Neither talked about being hurt or compromised by these people, which infers the respect these people have earned from Delilah and Macy.

Collegiality among administrators was deemed as important by those interviewed. As a principal, Matt noted the importance of the connections between his district's administrators. During administrative meetings or at conferences, he believed his team benefited from a relationship rooted in fun and humor. He felt his connection helped the administrators stay on the same page with district messaging and new initiatives even though they all reside at different buildings.

On the other side of this experience, as an associate principal Leo had very little contact with other administrators. His relationship with his supervisor was strong, but his district did not include associates in meetings. As a result, he was completely dependent on his principal for information. When pressed on the issue, Leo did not seem too concerned with this situation. Perhaps this is an issue with associate principals as Matt noted that in his own district, there had been a large turnover of associate principals. Leo's lack of contact with other administrators was not a source of negative tension, but he was learning about administration on his own.

A collective group is a valuable component of both CTE and alleviating negative tensions. Both formal and informal opportunities to be with people who have had similar experiences can be beneficial, so long as those instances do not get mired down in negativity. The teachers noted that to grow collegiality, teachers and administrators should look towards creating opportunities to confer with colleagues in order to get to know each other, determine possible solutions, hear the truth, and have fun.

TEACHER LEADERS

Nicole is teacher leader in her district's teachers' union and has had to take part in conversations with her administration regarding teaching and learning issues. Nicole doesn't like conflict and cites some of these conversations as hard or awkward. She realizes that even though she would not seek these types of conversations out herself she has an obligation to step into these moments because of her teacher leader role. She likes to resolve things as quickly as possible with colleagues and administrators and then be friends again.

Nicole's philosophy is if a person believes in something, he or she should lean into it, hence the reason she steps up for leadership roles in her professional life. But when colleagues approach her with issues they'd like her to present to her administrators, she has to make a judgment call as to whether it is an issue that should be addressed. At times she tries to deal with the people's concerns directly and let them know in a kind way that it's not a thing their administrators could, should, or would do anything about. She might sympathize with the person and help develop solutions the person could work with.

"Teacher leaders" are typically described as teachers who still have classroom duties in teaching students but take on additional duties outside of their classroom (Danielson, 2006). Teacher leadership roles can include both formal and informal positions. Teachers interviewed here held positions that included: curriculum team members, department heads, coaching, supervising clubs, mentoring colleagues, developers of courses, advanced education and certifications. They also held leadership roles in the community including literacy organizations, religious affiliations, sporting groups, and board members for various organizations.

The administrators looked for opportunities, when they could, to empower teachers in their schools as leaders, believing that when their teachers had a voice in decision-making they would be more likely to embrace and uphold the vision. There were different leadership styles among the principals. Two acted with methods consistent with distributed leadership where more people are welcome in the decision-making process. The remaining two principals veered towards top-down leadership where those at the apex of the school structure make the most decisions.

Interestingly, no administrators truly identified with "servant leadership," a style where the main goal is to be at the service of followers and help grow them into leaders. None of the administrators worked for schools at which they had previously taught or counseled, leaving one to assume they had to go outside of their district to gain leadership opportunities. On the flip side, no teachers intimated that they had to leave a district because of a lack of leadership opportunities.

Professional development leaders, book study group members, student assistance team members, and team leaders were the main teacher leadership roles these administrators provided for their teachers. Mitch, the high school principal, tried to give much decision-making power to his team leaders and committee members, something they had not experienced with previous administrators. He admits there was a rough period where teachers were not sure what to expect, and a year in which he had teachers who were not leadership material in positions. He was trying to determine ways to alleviate those issues.

Sometimes it is difficult to find teachers willing to put themselves in leadership roles. JoAnne's principal contacted specific members of his staff and told them he needed them to step up and lead in certain meetings. JoAnne was one of these people and she was eager to take on the role being requested of her. Likewise, as an administrator, Matt was struggling with finding enough teachers to attend a professional development conference. When only a few teachers volunteered, he felt that he was going to personally have to tell teachers in his building to take the remaining spots, something he was hesitant to do.

Finding teacher leaders who are willing and capable of taking on these roles involves administrators knowing their staff members' areas of strength. It also, to an extent, involves knowing teachers' weaknesses. It is important to take into consideration the extent of the task involved with the role. Is it for a long period of time? Is it a short initiative? Does it involve a lot of hours during or after the school day? These are things administrators should reflect on when having to find teachers for specific leader roles.

While administrators have the power to bestow leadership roles upon teacher leaders, these teachers, once selected, have a fine line to walk among their colleagues. Even though they are teachers, they may be looked at as outsiders to fellow educators. On the other hand, because they remain in the classroom, administrators often do not consider teacher leaders to be one of their own either. Teacher leaders took on positions of leadership for a variety of reasons: pay increase, a passion for the purpose, their own children would be involved, or because they felt a sense of duty.

It is therefore important for administrators and teacher leaders to make sure the person, purpose, and actions are in alignment. All of these factors must be thought through to help create a successful setting where a teacher leader can be successful. Teacher leaders help spread decision-making out so that one or two people are not making all the decisions for a school.

How do educators become teacher leaders? Growing administrators as leaders is a focus of many college programs, but developing teacher leaders is a relatively new concept. Organizations such as the Teacher Leadership Exploration Consortium (TLEC) have developed documents such as the Teacher Leader Model Standards (TLMS) as a way to explore what teacher leadership is and what competencies are necessary. Models and lists like these are tools schools, districts, and teachers can refer to when making decisions about who should hold leadership positions (Teacher Leadership Exploratory Consortium, 2011).

The TLMS domains include competencies that could be incorporated into teacher leadership expectations: providing support, using data, leading, collaborating with communities, and advocating for students. While not an implementation plan, the National Education Association, which helped develop the TLMS, says these are meant to instigate conversation about what teacher leadership is and can be (National Education Association 2020). Toolkits like the TLMS give districts a place to start when looking for teachers to take on leadership roles.

When utilized, teacher leadership can occur at different levels. The first is obviously within the classroom where teachers lead a group of students through learning activities to enhance their understanding. Among the teachers Delilah, Craig, and JoAnne all expressed desires for teachers to be entrusted with not only their classroom practices but to also be given opportunities to lead initiatives in their schools.

All had experienced situations in which they were told what to do in their content areas regardless of whether they agreed with the decisions or not. Delilah felt frustrated that her classroom practices were being decided by the adoption of a content program. Craig sensed the lack of trust in his abilities to take over a program he initially knew nothing about, and as a result was told to do things he felt would have been harmful to students' education. JoAnne felt a sense of anger when a curricular coach was hired to help her team. In all three instances, choices were being made for these teachers by entities outside of the classroom.

Teacher leadership can also be implemented in one of two ways. One path is with specific, identified leader roles in a building. This is known as "formal teacher leadership." The roles of teacher leaders can also occur organically, where teachers with natural interests or skills rise to the challenge taking on issues and duties. This is known as "informal teacher leadership." Teacher leaders interviewed rose to their positions in both ways.

Nicole described her participation in the teachers' union as a position where she communicated with both teachers and administration. Ariel was a team leader and felt her role was to be the intermediary between her team and her administrator, passing information along in both directions and helping to set up systems. Mitch discussed how he used his department heads to determine priorities. Other examples of formal teacher leadership included these as well as: curricular teams, school improvement groups, district initiatives, interview teams, coaches, and mentors.

"Informal teacher leadership," although this is a little more challenging to identify, occurred with our teachers as well. These are educators who step out without an official title but still fill voids, create a vision, or lead by being role models or sharing via professional development opportunities. Matt noted the importance of having teachers sign up for conferences to share information with staff. JoAnne's administrator contacted specific members of the school's staff take a leadership role when their strengths would be beneficial to a specific goal.

While it is more challenging to define these roles, schools need these types of educators who are willing to take on tasks or roles that help move the school towards its goals. Sometimes it happens naturally, and other times teachers may need to be nudged. Regardless of how it happens, acknowledging the teacher is an important component of both informal and formal teacher leadership. Delilah declared that teachers need to be recognized even if it irritates other teachers who are not stepping up. Craig felt strongly about the fact that administrators should trust and use the knowledge at their disposal.

COMMON GOALS

Macy feels that there are many demands in teaching. What frustrates Macy is the variety of expectations—some are known, unknown, clear, or unclear—and these can amplify an already challenging profession. The unclear demands, particularly, are exacerbated when expectations for situations are not specified and people in her school are not consistent with what is expected of students. She cites recess duty as being an example of this. She also sees this issue in the school's hallways and lunch room. She would like to have set parameters defining appropriate and inappropriate student behavior.

Curricularly, she feels there is a definite difference in the amount of time teachers spend preparing lessons for students. She acknowledged that it would be difficult to standardize lesson planning time, but wished for some guidance that could be utilized by all teachers. This lack of collective vision for expectations was cited by Macy as sources of negative tension. She feels it's important for everyone to be on the same page but doesn't think her building is quite there yet.

Clearly defined goals that a building staff can set its eyes to is an important component of collective efficacy. A common vision helps align purpose and focus for all groups. But, goals should be meaningful. Anne Conzemius, founder of the consulting organization QLD Learning, cites the need for quality goals as a means to intentionality (Conzemius, 2010). Goals must:

- Be developed collaboratively by those doing the work
- Reach beyond a year or two
- Address a few high-priority problems rather than many issues
- Speak to the whole organization
- Be aligned both vertically and horizontally, across grade levels and through grade levels

Both teachers and administrators viewed goal setting positively and negatively. If a goal was understood by the person being interviewed, then it was seen as a positive. Goals involving student achievement, school-wide discipline policies, and staff-wide professional development initiatives were cited as having positive impacts. However, goals that were not priorities for those interviewed were viewed less positively and added to the amount of negative tension experienced by teachers and administrators.

These included implementation of certain curricular programs, new sensitivity training for staff, and professional development opportunities where administrators had to force teachers to attend—either because no one expressed an interest or because it was a district-wide initiative. Reasons teachers were not in agreement with these included the method of implementation, the philosophy associated with it, or the feeling that they already possessed the skills that were being presented.

Again, there is a very fine line between allowing stakeholders to make decisions versus administrators. It is unclear from these interviews whether teachers wanted administrators to set the guidelines or if they wanted to be the ones to set their own goals. Instead, the tension seemed to arise from the fact that either no one was making the decisions or decisions were being made without teacher input.

Macy really needed her school to have common expectations for student behavior; the variety between teachers was in her view a problem. JoAnne wanted all of her colleagues to be pushed to become the strong teachers she felt they could be. Jeff wanted clarification regarding expectations for special education students: What is the school's vision when it comes to taking tests? On the other hand, Delilah was in the midst of a disagreement with administrators regarding content that she and her colleagues needed to implement in their classrooms.

Macy admitted that there is that fine line between dictating what needs to be done versus general guidelines; she doesn't want all decisions to be made for her, but there are areas she definitely believes the teachers need to know the minimum expectation. JoAnne agreed with this as well; she intimated that the level of rigor, particularly for special education students, needed to be raised in her school.

So who do educators look to in order to create that shared vision? In all of these instances it was administrators. Teachers were looking to their principals, mostly, to set the goals. In situations where administrators were not addressing their concerns, teachers cited these issues as sources of tension. To be fair, some administrators were made aware of the situation and some had not been told about them. So first, teachers need to tell administrators when tensions arise if they would like their administrators to address their concerns.

Some interviewees, however, discussed the possibility of teachers setting their own goals, particularly when teacher leadership was an asset valued by school principals. Mitch noted that when his teachers had the ability to make goals in his school there was more buy-in by staff to anything new. When he became principal, he had some teachers leave his school because they didn't subscribe to his vision, but he believes that now he has a staff that feels empowered and believes in the goals.

Teacher Jeff pointed to his school's PLCs (Professional Learning Community) as an opportunity for groups of teachers to gather and set a common vision. As a grade level team leader, Ariel facilitated her team's decision-making regarding system level expectations during biweekly meetings. JoAnne discussed the value of her team gathering during the school day to work through differences of opinions regarding content-area lessons.

Giving teachers time and, most importantly, the permission to determine common goals in an authentic way empowers them to not only take care of each other but to also take a lead in solving a school's problems. Administrators do need to make decisions, but utilizing tools such as the TLMS while giving teachers formal or informal time to meet helps grow teachers' abilities as problem solvers with a purpose.

RESPONSIVE LEADERS WHO SHOW CONCERN FOR THEIR STAFF

Finally, having an administrator who is responsive to the concerns of staff is important in CTE, but also to the teachers interviewed here. While there is no direct correlation between the leadership style of administrators and each teacher's level of negative tension, principals' actions were seen to have an impact on both the day-to-day functions of a teacher's life and in the long term.

Jeff cited an incident where his district initiated a year-long professional development series that was not functioning as it should; small groups met once a month, people weren't seeing the value in the development, and the expectations were not aligned with what was actually happening in school. A few months into the initiative, after hearing feedback from his teachers, the principal decided that he was going to restructure the professional development. Instead of using various after-school times, he set the meeting times so teachers would meet during the school day within the staff's schedule.

The entire staff would meet together but work in small groups in the same room versus being segmented and away from each other in different areas of the building. Jeff stated that it was more palatable to take part in the professional development in this manner. Jeff cites the fact that his principal took in staff members' perspectives and created a solution they could all live with, versus being the enforcer, was much more successful than it would have been if adjustments had not been made.

Teachers looked to their administrators for guidance on all sorts of educational matters. Principals admitted they have a lot of situations to deal with in a day, and teachers acknowledged they knew their issue was not always the most important. But having an administrator listen to a problem and then work to rectify it was viewed positively by teachers.

Relationships between administrators and teachers could change depending on the time or the topic. JoAnne's relationship with her principal began negatively, but she appreciated that he listened to her concerns and got to know her as a person. Delilah had a tenuous relationship with one of her administrators because she did not feel she could approach this person regarding certain issues but was comfortable discussing other pressing matters.

On the other end of the spectrum, Craig had a principal early in his career who did an observation in his classroom where a student sat with her head down most of class. Instead of docking Craig points during his observation, the principal asked Craig to talk about the situation. Craig was able to explain that this student was slowly adapting to school and that she did not yet have the stamina for a full class period. This led to an open discussion about helping students who struggle in various forms. Craig felt heard. And he spoke fondly of this some twenty years later.

Having responsive leaders who show concern for their staff is a part of CTE, a needed component in developing a group of stakeholders who believe they can achieve desired outcomes or goals. Additionally, people in decision-making roles would benefit from listening to the people who are doing the work. It is difficult to solve a problem without a true sense of what the issues are. Since administrators cannot be everywhere at all times, listening to staff and allowing them to help make decisions has a powerful impact on a school's goals being authentic and viewed as necessary.

T. J. Hoogsteen writes that creating a group with strong collective efficacy involves steps (Hoogsteen, 2020): goal setting, collaboration, goal monitoring, celebrations when the group has reached mastery. These components are what the teachers here have pointed to as strategies that can either alleviate or add to negative tension. The process of growing CTE needs to be organic but explicit. A strong sense of CTE can change the negative tensions from being the concern of one solitary teacher alone in a classroom to the responsibility of the entire group.

During his time with an administrator who did not support him, Craig lost confidence and his sense of self. His colleagues did not know him as a person nor understand his areas of expertise. It was during this time that he read a magazine article cautioning people to not forget who they are. This awakened in Craig the reminder of his purpose—to get better at his job and help those around him improve their practice.

Craig says this forced him to find his "tribe." He made himself more visible to his colleagues and helped them understand his role but also showed how he could help them. He found Twitter to be a useful tool to make connections with others as he gravitated towards certain hashtags and began to follow like-minded people. He attended conferences. Additionally, because another administrator knew Craig's skill set, she stepped in and helped him navigate the dangerous administrative decisions he was being asked to implement.

Eventually, the entire administrative team in Craig's school was transferred out and his school began what he called a "clean slate." A new structure was designated for the school and the entire staff had the whole summer to meet and determine the school's vision. Not having the protocols and procedures from the previous year caused negative tension for Craig and his colleagues, but he noted that while the tension itself was negative, the results led to positive outcomes. His program had expectations and goals. He was part of a staff that had a vision and common goals, and he knew where his program fit within the larger system.

How do teachers and administrators protect each other from negative tension? First, each individual needs to see themselves as part of the collective whole put in charge of creating a strong academic environment for students in their charge. Every individual in this group has various skill sets that they should explore opportunities to lead, whether formally or informally or even beyond what is expected, in order to move the group forward.

But, without clear goals, the group doesn't know the target to shoot for. In addition, teacher leaders should be given the ability to help make the goals and set expectations for the building; administrators should not have to feel like they need to make all the decisions in a school. And finally, when an administrator is able to be responsive to the needs of his or her staff, it is possible to make adjustments that reduce any negative tensions increased by a situation. Listening, asking questions, helping staff uncover their strengths, and being willing to make changes are traits the teachers in the study appreciated in their administrators.

REFLECTIVE QUESTIONS

1. What is the level of collective efficacy in your group?
2. What are the strengths of your group in terms of collective efficacy?
3. What areas of weakness does your group have in terms of collective efficacy?
4. If you were to help your group's level of collective efficacy, where would you start?

REFERENCES

Bandura, Albert. (1998). "Personal and Collective Efficacy in Human Adaptation and Change." In *Advances in Psychological Science: Vol. 1. Personal, Social and Cultural Aspects*, ed. J. G. Adair, D. Belanger, and K. L. Dion (pp. 51–71). Psychology Press.

Conzemius, Anne E. (2010). "A Minimalist Approach to Reform." *The School Administrator* 67(1). https://www.aasa.org/SchoolAdministratorArticle.aspx?id=11114.

Danielson, Charlotte. (2006). *Teacher Leadership That Strengthens Professional Practice*. ASCD.

Donohoo, J. A. M. (2016). *Collective Efficacy: How Educators' Beliefs Impact Student Learning* (1st ed.). Corwin.

Hattie, John. (2019). "Watch John Hattie's Keynote on Collaborative Impact." Visible Learning, April 5, 2019. https://visible-learning.org/2017/05/video-john-hattie-collaborative-impact/.

Hoogsteen, T. J. (2020). "Collective Efficacy: Toward a New Narrative of Its Development and Role in Achievement." *Palgrave Communications* 6(2). https://doi.org/10.1057/s41599-019-0381-z.

National Education Association. (2020). "The Teacher Leader Model Standards." https://www.nea.org/resource-library/teacher-leader-model-standards.

Teacher Leadership Exploratory Consortium. (2011). "Teacher Leader Model Standards." https://www.ets.org/s/education_topics/teaching_quality/pdf/teacher_leader_model_standards.pdf.

Chapter 7

The Path of Enlightenment

Hopefully, the tensions presented here are ones that many educators can relate to. Most likely those in education have found aspects of the tensions, or situations similar that are consistent across multiple different educational environments. It is important to note that these tensions exist across schools and across contexts. What can vary is the reaction individuals have to that. Due to the uncomfortable nature of tensions, for many experiencing tension, this results in weight gain or a bad mood. Which brings us back to tensions being like that exercise band, stretching us to improve.

However, according to research by Boe et al. (2008), nearly 40 percent of new teachers will leave the profession by the end of their fifth year of teaching. While this happens for a variety of reasons, many factors that have been studied, and are currently being studied, lead us to believe that tensions have a role in this burnout rate. This attrition rate dramatically decreases beyond those early years (drops to a 15 percent), which signals that teachers learn to cope, learn to address and understand the issues that cause tension in their profession, even if they cannot name them. In all of this research, the causes of burnout typically relate to stress and pressure in the profession.

Yet, tension can be both of these things. Therefore, tension has a natural spot in this conversation. Hopefully by continuing to understand our responses to these tensions, we will find additional ways to support our new teachers and administrators in the profession, leading to a decline in the flight from the profession.

This chapter is not, however, meant to focus on the negative effects of tension on the profession. Instead, this chapter will first recognize the positive tensions, and impact of positive tensions. Then it will look at how teachers learn to cope with tensions in order to be productive in their educational environments.

TENSIONS CAN BE POSITIVE, THEY REALLY CAN

We believe that tensions CAN be a positive thing. If we approach tensions as the idea of situations, pressures, and experiences that will challenge, push, and motivate change, then the sure premise of the idea of tension will be positive in nature. As Leo puts it: "I think that they're all positive in some respects because they're all pushing me to be better, to think differently, to present my ideas better, to challenge what my values are and how I am communicating with the staff, so I believe that they are all positive."

Yet, for most, the initial reaction of people when they hear and talk about tension it is an anxiety-inducing idea. For each of our participants, when they rebranded the idea of tensions to apply them to their experiences, they all inserted terms like stress, pressure, anxiety, challenges as they relate to tension. Each of these words and concepts has a negative connotation to it.

Jeff describes the idea of switching his thinking on tensions by saying: "We talk with our students about when they work to the edge of their learning and they're in that zone of discomfort that's where you grow the most." This is what he believes tensions are similar to. Oftentimes, those experiences that are beyond our comfort zone create moments of tension, but once we confront them and adjust for them, we are able to grow through them.

We aim to highlight the positive aspects of tensions. We will do this through looking at how tensions have improved the environment for schools through common understanding, boosting student experiences, and relationship building.

TENSION TO CREATE A COMMON UNDERSTANDING

Tensions that result in a common understanding of a situation or curriculum are beneficial to continued effective communication practices. Quite frequently, tensions arise when there are different perspectives on a situation or experience. This could be between teacher and student, or teacher and colleague/teacher, and frequently between administrator and teachers. Tension increases when these groups are immersed in the same school and are confronted with the same situation, but have differing views on it due to a breakdown in communication.

These tensions are oftentimes quite stressful and anxiety-filled. However, when that tension results in a productive conversation, it allows all parties to come to an understanding on the actions and responses that led to that tension. As JoAnne recognized: "Good tensions are when you're learning something (together)." When multiple parties come together to learn more about one another while also learning about the situation, they are able to move into resolution of those tensions much quicker.

Mitch shares: "Having that tough conversation with somebody may not feel real good at the time but it's a coaching conversation that helps push some thinking, ultimately, (which) I think ends up being positive." If the two work together to build understanding of one another, then more likely than not, that tension will not be as great if it occurs again. This is due to the fact that the two will approach situations with a new understanding of one another, which will allow them to use that knowledge as new situations arise. The new understanding should diminish the tensions that each part feels. And as Leo said, once we have reached the positive response to a tension, then "you can move forward" working well with one another.

TENSION TO BOOST STUDENT EXPERIENCES

Mitch very directly states that "any tensions that end up resulting in better conditions for students to succeed are positive." This positions tensions as a system that creates change in the educational environment. It also indicates that it is sometimes important to live in a space of tension if, in the end, it will result in a better situation for the students. While this text has already previously recognized that living in tensions is uncomfortable, and creates additional stress, it also shared successful ways of managing and dealing with these tensions.

The impact of the change is in direct relationship to how that tension is handled, reflected on, and learned from. Some tensions, the particularly stressful ones, make it difficult to process and reflect on, as there can be trauma that occurs due to that tension. In time, that tension will still need to be understood in order for any change to occur. This is easier done in conjunction with others, specifically a support system.

Craig shared his experience working through a tension with a colleague: "Talk about positive tension—we were able to reduce that tension in a very collaborative way and I think that's one of the best ways to make them feel heard." Allowing the learning process to be one in tandem with a colleague allows for both of the educators to not only feel heard, but also understood, and supported. Oftentimes tensions are something that are handled through reflection on their own. However, when that tension is brought forward, when it is acknowledged and worked through jointly with others, it allows for continued growth for multiple people.

Again, this isn't always easy.

Mitch reflects on it by saying: "The positive tensions are the ones that result in positive outcomes for students and so by backing off of those conversations, even though you might risk a relationship here and there, if we are really in this for the students I think we have to have those conversations and trust one another that it's not personal and that I am still going to support you but we have to think about this differently." Meaning, it is okay to step back, take time for the personal reflection, but then come to the table ready and willing to work together to figure out the tension and, hopefully, lessen the tension in order to make a better environment for the students.

Speaking of students, not only is it okay, but it is also sometimes appropriate to include the students into the processing of tensions in the classroom, particularly when it involves them. Including the students into the growth situation shows them the flexibility of the educator, but also that the educator is willing to learn and grow, creating learning environments the best that they can be.

Showing students the process of managing tensions is a healthy life lesson, and reminds them that we all experience tensions in different ways and it is our responses that really matter. While there are many times where it might not be appropriate to include students into the process, including them in the learning opportunity, due to the tension, is an important experience for students to learn to cope and deal with situations that create tension.

Additionally, working through tensions that arise due to curriculum decisions creates a more supportive curriculum and learning environment. Delilah described a situation where she found the previous practices to be restrictive to meeting the needs of all of her students. She discussed:

> The practices were put in place a few years before I started, and just maintained. However, a few of the books that we were reading, and activities that went along with them, were not ones that met the needs of my current students, nor were they responsive to the class. This created a tension for me because I went against the current practice (and other teachers on my team) in order to fit my class and my students.

The tension here was one of restrictive educational practices, something that happens on a regular basis in educational environments.

Delilah chose to embrace the tension in order to provide a better experience for her students, even if this meant challenging her colleagues, or going against the curriculum that was provided to her. Yet, she knew that in the end, the experience that she was giving to her students would be much more beneficial and inclusive to their abilities and their needs, which in turn allows for a greater educational experience.

RELATIONSHIP BUILDING

Finally, one of the greatest benefits of tensions is the improved relationships that CAN occur in working through tensions with others. While we very much recognize that tensions left unresolved can break down relationships, we want to highlight that when these tensions are resolved, when they are handled, it can allow for relationships to strengthen and grow.

Jeff talked about relationships growing with his administration through the evaluation process. For many, this evaluation process can be a tension-inducing process. Many teachers, who are being evaluated by their administration, feel anxious and the need for things to be perfect. They want to be "judged" as competent and successful. Therefore, the administration's response to the evaluation can either increase or alleviate tensions.

Craig discussed the process of the follow-up evaluation being about the conversation that takes place with the administration. He felt that his evaluation process "forces us to have a conversation rather than just a checkbox." This allows his administration to get to know him and the decisions he makes when teaching, rather than just watching the output of those decisions.

Craig followed up by saying, "When you've got a relationship that's healthy and somebody you can trust, that is what really determines whether it is a positive tension or a negative tension. The negative is that there's no relationship or desire to have one and that causes harmful tension." This emphasizes how trust is a major factor in managing tensions in the relationship.

Lack of trust results in tensions that are often not resolved and allowed to escalate. Relationships that do have trust are typically able to have constructive conversations, resulting in tensions alleviated and a learning experience for all.

Matt found that living in tension with others allowed for additional relationship building among his team. Matt described a situation where he had to work with others through a particularly stressful situation. He said: "I think that really pulled us together because we had to do things consistently. We had to make sure messages were consistent because otherwise everyone was looking to us—'how are you going to do this?'" These relationships were built due to their need to be consistent with each other, but also because they turned to one another in support of the tension.

This is one of the reasons why having a community of thinkers, and a support system, is so important, and why many of our participants recognized their ability to manage tensions due to that support system. It is particularly helpful if that support system is experiencing the same tensions. Conversation and collaboration are able to occur to manage and cope with those tensions, working to lessen the impact of that tension.

YOU CAN MANAGE THIS WITHOUT WEIGHT GAIN

We have found that many of our participants have physical reactions to these tensions. One stated: "Just . . . you get warm in the face, you feel anger and frustration welling up, and my hands would literally shake." Another said: "I gain weight because I stress eat. It was really hard. I cried." Both of these are natural reactions to dealing with and handling stress. Both of these reactions are typical to many moments in our lives when we feel uncomfortable, challenged, or under pressure for something.

This experience as it relates to tension is not a novel idea. In fact, we can go as far as to include tension in the conversation of early teacher burnout. Research by Szczygieł supports this idea by recognizing that "individual negative emotional and health consequences further translate into social and economic costs—it has been proven that chronic stress makes it difficult to establish and maintain positive and satisfactory relations with other people, reduces work efficiency, leads to high staff turnover and losses caused by sickness absenteeism" (Szczygieł, 2020).

We want to give you the name of these tensions, recognize how they manifest in an educational environment, and the impact that it has on teaching. It is in doing this that we do not look to present the solution to these tensions, but rather help you to recognize what they are, and reflect on how tensions manifest themselves in your own educational environment.

So, back to how we started this section. We want to look at how to understand and approach tensions without the weight gain, and the emotional roller coaster associated with negative responses to tensions. We will do that by looking at how experienced educators shared their growth from their early years; we will look at how our educators shared how they cope with their tensions; and, finally, we will look at the benefits of finding your community of thinkers.

WHAT THEY'VE LEARNED

Each of the people that we talked to recognized that they were not always well equipped to handle tensions in their lives, much less their educational environments, particularly at the onslaught of their educational careers. Mitch said, speaking on his early career, "Normally you would just sit down at your desk and cry 'now what am I going to do?'" Craig said that he would just fall on the floor and want to stay there. For many, this initial reaction to tension is to avoid, to hide from it, and to let it consume them.

Many of the teachers and administrators we talked with discuss this notion of letting it consume and overwhelm them. Delilah talks about the fact that when tensions are particularly stressful, she feels it getting in the way of her interactions with her students. How she finds herself with a shorter fuse for negative behaviors that might arise, or her flexibility in renegotiating a lesson going poorly. This is due to the fact that her attention and focus are split between the tension and her immediate situation.

Leo recognized, "I think early on in my career coming into my office I would see that little red light on my voice message and that used to give me a little anxiety." The dreaded, red light! One that every teacher, administrator, and support person has experienced. The knowledge that on the other end of that red light is an unknown, a concern, a potential to change their effectiveness for their entire day.

Intrinsically, many associate that red light with a problem, an issue, something that they did wrong. The anticipation of that challenge on the other end of the voicemail is enough to create tension for all. And it does not matter if it is an experienced educator, or a new educator.

Usually, the idea of the unknown continues to create tension. The unknown results in a lack of control, which for many is a tension-inducing situation. While this tension is easy to lessen, by listening to the voicemail and communicating with the sender, it is just one example of where tensions can be created based on our own intrinsic expectation.

Nicole talked about the fact that for her, many of her tensions are due to pressures that are self-driven, especially early on in her career. She discussed having an "ego" when she started, a sense that everything had to be just right so that she could be an exceptional educator. This includes in her lesson planning, interacting with families, as well as returning grading.

Her need to have things just right, especially in the early years of teaching, created lots of tensions and negative feelings when things were going well. Similar to Nicole, Macy said how this need to have curriculum lined up and have the resources for students led her to spending a lot of time with it, and making sure that she knew it really well to be able to teach it well. All of that extra time, she admits, created a tension for her, because it took away from other outside-of-school activities that she wanted to do.

However, both Nicole and Macy have recognized that with years of teaching under their belt: "Some of it is not having the sense of ego that I had when I was first starting out," and that "I try now to be gentler with myself and remind myself that I don't have to do it all right away." Nicole wraps it up by saying: "I definitely think they decrease over time partly because the longer you are in any profession the more tools you have in your kit to deal with some of those things . . . you grow a thicker skin."

This "growing of thicker (referenced as tougher by others) skin," as multiple other participants have described it, has allowed the teachers to recognize the tension-inducing situations and find effective ways and tools to be able to handle those tensions.

When the teachers were experiencing greater levels of tension and did not have coping mechanisms for dealing with them, it impacts their mental well-being. For many, they described what Jeff describes as the lack of "being able to leave it at school." The tension lives with them, they dwell on the tension and it filters into other aspects of their lives. Jeff goes on to describe how certain tensions can really get to him, how his typical stress relievers are unable to quell the tension: "(I'm) getting run down by the process, the things that would normally energize me are just not getting it done anymore."

Research by Szczygieł recognizes the importance of understanding this mental impact on teachers particularly. It says: "The mental well-being of teachers is, in particular, in the public interest. It is directly linked to the quality of their work for their pupils and the local community as a whole. Even the best prepared teachers will teach and educate in a less effective way if their functioning at work is not optimal" (Szczygieł, 2020). Szczygieł recognizes that our effectiveness in an educational setting depends on our ability to recognize, name, control, and respond to stress and tensions.

This research goes on to show that when educational professionals are in a negative mental space, they lack the ability to form strong relationships, both with their students and with their colleagues. Oftentimes, this results in negative mental health and a disconnect with the people they work with the most. Therefore, according to this research, negative mental health trickles down to impacting the students.

With that said, it is important that teachers are able to recognize the major factors that have created these tensions for them, which tensions "stick" with them, and what efforts can best help to alleviate them. Hopefully the previous chapters presented tensions that you can connect to, both in the circumstances and the tensions, and have a better understanding of the tensions that exist in educational settings. Now we need to look at how to cope with them in order to support the health of educational environments.

HOW THEY COPE

To begin, the learning to cope with tensions was, and is not, an overnight process. While the research at the start of this chapter discussed the attrition rates in the first five years of teaching, it doesn't mean that by that sixth year everything is magically better. There will be, and are, tensions always present. And even the most experienced teachers and administrators will continue to wrestle with them. However, there are resources, methods, and efforts that help educators work through these tensions. For many of our educators and administrators, they recognized that the greatest tool they used to overcome this tension was time.

For Paula it is a matter of literally taking a break. She noted that she takes care of herself by stepping back. She stated: "I'm closed for business, do what you need to do, I'll tell you when I'm opened up for business." This allows her to reflect, to breathe, and to be her best self with her students. When she could treat the situation with a business model, she realized that she was able to take the steps she needed to be successful. Oftentimes she used this "closed for business" structure to just compose herself, take attendance, and position herself in her best place for teaching the class.

As mentioned in the previous section, Paula is recognizing her need to gauge her mental well-being here in order to be the best for her students. She knows that to be effective in connecting with her students, it is okay to allow her students to pause and be patient once in a while, in order for them all to move forward in a productive fashion. Paula often related aspects of her class to a business model. A "closed for business" stance shows the students that mental health, taking a break, and responding to stress is a regular part of your life, and important to healthy living.

For Matt, it means closing his office door and separating himself from the chaos of a busy day: "I like to separate myself from the situation or be in a private place so . . . I could process and then get back to it." Matt noted that his separation from others takes him out of the limelight for a moment. He does not have to worry about being watched for his reaction, but also doesn't have to be concerned with worrying those who would be watching.

Matt needs this time on his own to process, evaluate, and make a decision on how to respond and who to loop in. This recognition that his tensions are best resolved on his own helps him from escalating a current or future situation.

He knows that when he can close his door, sit quietly, he can come to a resolution much quicker. This is due to the fact that he does not let others impact his response to tension. Oftentimes, when too many people have an idea on how a situation or tension should be handled, it only results in an escalation of that tension. Taking the time to be quiet, to understand what has been the cause of the tension, who that tension impacts, and what his role should be in that tension, allows Matt to decide how to respond appropriately.

Macy noted the importance of positive self-reflection and talking through a specific tension. She noted: "Normally that's when I feel like I need to talk to myself. I'm telling myself to just breathe; they're not doing this on purpose. They are not doing this to make you upset. And then I try to figure out how they are seeing this in their minds." Her moment of pausing, and running through the scenario, allows her to examine the root cause, and be intentional before reacting.

This empathetic response recognizes that tension is a two-way street—she aims to understand the other person before making any decisions. It also allows her to step back from the situation and fully understand it before she allows it to create added tensions.

For Matt it is all about exercise and routine. He finds that when he is dealing with tensions at school, he is most effective if he can go about his typical routine, keeping things as normal as possible. Then, after school, he makes sure to take the time to exercise and process the tension while he is working out. During this time, he sets his plan for dealing with the tension, or letting it just pass. It is the next day where he plans to have the tough conversations that he needs to have.

Matt knows that he needs time to work through the tension, and a part of that time is to step aside, not react to the emotion of the tension in the moment, but instead take time to process and understand it, then set a plan for dealing with it. Matt is well aware of what will keep him both physically and mentally healthy, and he uses this blend when it comes to coping with tensions in his educational environment.

Each of the above responses is different in its approach to dealing with the tensions in the educational environment. Research shows that how a person copes with or deals with tension and stress is directly related to that person's physical, psychological, and emotional well-being (Endler and Parker, 1990). Therefore, along with understanding the tensions that are in your life, it is also important to recognize how these tensions are processed and dealt with.

"Based on the results of the 'Multidimensional Inventory for Measuring Coping with Stress,' 15 styles of stress management are listed. The styles have been divided based on N. S. Endler and J. D. A. Parker—Task-oriented, Emotional-oriented, avoidance-oriented" (Szczygieł, 2020). When we look at the responses presented above, each can fit into one of these categories.

The research goes on to say: "Teachers most often use the most constructive style of dealing with stress, namely they are task-oriented in their remedial actions. . . . Relatively high results were also obtained on the scale of emotional style. . . . Least frequently the surveyed teachers declare that they take evasive actions in a stressful situation" (Szczygieł, 2020). This aligns with the responses that our participants shared.

We found that many of the shared responses started with taking a step back before forming a plan for supporting, and coping, with the tension as it existed. While we saw responses that included the emotional in terms of immediate reactions, we found that the teachers moved into an action response to those reactions. This could be the personalities of the educators that we worked with, or a general reaction that aligns with the profession, both of which are similar to what Endler and Parker found.

COMMUNITY OF THINKERS

One common trend that we heard each of our participants discuss in how they handle tensions in their educational environments is through establishing a community of like-minded colleagues and "thinkers" in order to talk through the tension and situation that those teachers and administrators are in. As previously demonstrated in this chapter, establishing a community for conversation is vital to the health of an organization, education specifically. Henry Seton (2019) recognizes a growing issue in the education profession. He describes it as:

> We wondered silently to ourselves if we were up to the challenge. We quietly congratulated ourselves on every school year we completed, as if we had just survived the Hunger Games. We maybe even secretly took pride that we weren't the colleague regularly in tears in the staff room. We became numb to other people's stress. (Seton, 2019, p. 78)

Due to this numbing of our feelings, teachers allow tensions and stress to hold greater space in their mental health, which is not a productive practice. Therefore, we present ways that our participants find their community, their group from whom to seek guidance and support. Each of our participants discussed their community of thinkers in different ways. Some sought solace from co-workers at their schools, others found them at home. And finally, some of the participants found that their greatest community of thinkers were through online platforms and social media.

Nicole and Jeff both found themselves confiding with their co-workers. Nicole said that many of her tensions are discussed at their lunch tables. Specifically, she said: "Having other people get it and commiserate with you helps." She also noted that it does not become a situation of only negative talk, but the chance to discuss and talk through some of the tensions helps her to move past them. Similarly, Jeff shares his tensions with his colleagues. He admitted that it wasn't always easy; at the start he was quite self-conscious about it. He noted:

> Just knowing that even though (they) may be older, they're more established or whatever it might be, that you know your opinion is your opinion and you're entitled to it and they might not like it, they might not take your ideas, they might not resolve it but that, probably for the most part, they'll at least respect that you have that opinion.

Jeff recognizes the importance of seeking guidance from his colleagues with more experience, but also that he gains their respect by speaking up, looking for their thoughts, while also sharing his own thoughts and opinions. He also believes that because of these conversations, problem solving, and banter, that his school seems like a family. This is a good thing for him, as a difference in opinion is a natural part of being a family.

He believes this helps not only diffuse tensions, but support him in his teaching. He says, "I've always sort of felt that the teaching community was sort of a family you know, and I came from a big family so we don't always get along, we don't always see each other's ways, but generally there's a feeling like we're all in it together." Which allows them to find the best solution to tensions between colleagues as well as students.

Leo also consults with his principal quite regularly. He has noted that his own approach to situations is quite different from that of his principal, so when he is struggling with a situation, he seeks her thoughts and advice. This, he feels, provides a well-rounded thought on the tensions. As an administrator himself, he feels that this step is important as it relates to finding the best way, the "perfect words" for supporting the students at his school, and other teachers through these tensions.

Others like Matt, JoAnne, and Macy turn to their friends and family. Matt shared that he and his wife drive home together and that they typically will choose a spot on their ride that they can talk about school until. Once they hit that spot they transition to their family. He said that the space of talking about school with a boundary is helpful as it restricts taking too much home with them.

Same thing with Macy. She stated how important it is that "you seek out people to talk to. Sometimes you just need to vent." And that her family often becomes these people for her. This allows her to get the tension off of her chest, expressing it out loud, and thinking about how it sounds. This helps her understand the gravity of the tension, or if it is something that she can move past.

JoAnne finds that her best friend becomes this person. She appreciates having her best friend in the same district, just different buildings, to understand the district's expectations, but that she still does a lot of "whining and complaining" to her, especially as it comes to tensions at school. Whether it is friends or family, having sounding boards is helpful in dealing with tensions, especially, unlike JoAnne's, if they are a bit more removed from the situation. This space allows for added objectivity, and a safe space to discuss situations that are particularly filled with tension.

Finally, there were multiple people who responded to finding their community of thinkers through anonymity. They turned to platforms online specifically for educators to find inspiration and support. Leo said he turned to

Twitter to "get some of those more inspirational messages and different ways of framing my mindset in the moment." His ability to find a group online allows Leo to not worry about who knows who. No names are mentioned, but rather scenarios are discussed, and Leo is able to get multiple perspectives on how to handle that same scenario.

Then he is able to use the thoughts of the collective group in helping him formulate his direction for handling the tension. The other benefit for seeking support on an online platform is that it reaches a much broader audience, and many of that group can relate to the tensions presented. This reminds Leo, and many other educators, that they are not alone in these tensions, and that they occur in a variety of educational settings. Simply the knowledge of community, the knowledge of not being alone, helps to make these tensions much more manageable.

So, it does not matter if your supporters are your colleagues, family and friends, or other platforms for conversation. What matters is that conversations are taking place as they relate to mental health, and tensions in the educational environment. Research shows: "It is essential that we extend compassion to ourselves, our students, and our colleagues by addressing the elephant in the room of teacher mental health" (Seton, 2019, p. 80).

Tensions are tough. However, they are not all negative. This chapter explored how tensions can be positive, how they can challenge practices that might be outdated and harmful to students. They also showed how they can build relationships with colleagues and students based on your responses to those tensions when you are ready to open yourself up to include others in the solving of those tensions. Tensions that are solved in conjunction with others allow for optimal growth, mostly because it allows multiple people to grow and learn from that tension.

As described, learning from tensions is something that happens through experience in education. All of our participants recognized that they have gotten better at managing their tensions throughout the years of teaching. Along with finding a support system, or a community of thinkers, going through tension allows you to add to the tools you have for managing those tensions in the future. Leo describes this aspect of tensions in a similar fashion as we presented early on in the book. He said:

> It's challenging, it's challenging me to do better, it's kind of like the resistance band training. As you begin to minimize tensions and take off those resistance bands, (I'm) building up those strengths, I'm going to be able to handle more situations.

While the idea of tension brings up reactions of stress and anxiety, it is important to recognize the good that comes from managing tensions. It allows you to focus your attention on growth from the tension. Each tension that you experience will bring forward new ways to manage and react to that tension, and, in the end, will add to your repertoire of tools to help you feel successful in dealing with tensions.

REFLECTIVE QUESTIONS

1. What is your typical reaction when tensions arise?
2. What is your support system (your community of thinkers) who bring varied perspectives to helping you understand and manage tensions?
3. How have you grown as an educator and professional due to managing tensions?

REFERENCES

Boe, Erling E., Lynne H. Cook, and Robert J. Sunderland. (2008). "Teacher Turnover: Examining Exit Attrition, Teaching Area Transfer, and School Migration." *Exceptional Children* 75(1): 7–31.

Endler, N. S., and J. D. Parker. (1990). "Multidimensional Assessment of Coping: A Critical Evaluation." *Journal of Personality and Social Psychology* 58(5): 844–854. https://doi.org/10.1037//0022-3514.58.5.844.

Seton, Henry. (2019). "The Elephant in the Classroom." *Educational Leadership* 77(2): 77–80.

Szczygieł, Magdalena. (2020). "Stress at the Teacher's Workplace—Chosen Factors." *Culture - Society - Education* 2(18): 331–349. https://pressto.amu.edu.pl/index.php/kse/article/download/28000/25368.

Chapter 8

Now What?

NEW LENS ON TENSION

There is a common phrase: "Life is what you make of it." Well, what if tensions are thought about in a similar fashion? Meaning, can educators embrace tensions for being a positive aspect in their jobs, in their professional growth, in their lives? The previous chapter presented the ways that tensions can have positive outcomes. This chapter will further present the perspectives on tensions, the thinking and justification on why tensions can BE positive, not just have positive outcomes. Living in tensions is uncomfortable; tensions result in increased stress and anxiety, and they can encourage negative physical reactions. But what is the root cause, the fact that they are uncontrollable, often unanticipated?

Many tensions are due to the unpredictable nature of them, the fact that tensions between individuals are the result of unanticipated reactions. The thing is, that will always be the case. One will never hit a point where others are always predictable and controlled. That is the beauty of human nature. This chapter hopes to inspire a reframing of consideration on tensions—that one can name those tensions, understand what it is that is causing the stress, and help educators move into their management strategies of these tensions.

AWARENESS!

When someone is experiencing tensions, the ability to know how to name them as they are happening allows someone to understand the situation and move towards progress instead of getting stuck in the stress stage of the tension. Hopefully, naming that tension as it occurs creates a new understanding for the environment and situation. Through the naming process, reflection occurs to recognize why this is causing tension and what led up to it. Sometimes just being able to step back and say "this is a tension in my life right now" allows the person to recognize the temporary nature and move into their coping mechanisms.

Delilah recognized: "(I) used to sit in that tension. I would stew about the situation and I would replay what led to it. Oftentimes thinking about where I went wrong—that it led to this." Without being able to name the tension, Delilah gets stuck in the space of it. What if she were to be able to acknowledge what it was, recognize the anxiety as a tension at an early stage, then be able to move into her management strategies for coping with it? As previously identified, there are many ways to cope with tensions.

These strategies are similar to coping with stress in a situation and environment. But a different understanding occurs when one is able to step back, recognize that they are experiencing tension, and move right into the reflection aspect of it. The reflection should include the mentality that tensions can be positive, with a lot of room for personal growth from the situation. Therefore, a change in framing in regard to thinking about tensions should allow a new understanding of the tension (dare we say embrace it) and unlock the ability to learn from it.

NO WAY TO ELIMINATE

The work with tensions is to become aware of their presence and impacts on our lives. As discussed, a major impact is to learn how to grow from them, and be better the next time that we encounter them. But the plain fact of the matter is, an individual will never be completely free of tensions. Many would wish that the work and discussion regarding tensions would allow us to completely alleviate tensions from our lives.

Unfortunately, this is just not possible. Both human nature and the sheer structure of the educational system mean that educators will never be able to fully rid tensions from their lives. But the reasons that make this impossible are also why most people love teaching.

TENSIONS WITH CONSTANTLY CHANGING STUDENTS

Most of the tensions experienced are due to interactions with the students. These tensions can be hidden or visible, they can involve the student or not. But the thing is, because the population is always growing and changing, educators will constantly be presented with the same tensions as well as new tensions.

For example, Nicole discussed a student whose personality and lack of engagement created quite a bit of tension in her classroom and in her teaching practices. Nicole did whatever she could do to alleviate that tension with that student, found the strategies she needed in order to motivate this student, and help the student feel more successful in the classroom. This is great; this tension is quelled. However, it is a guarantee that Nicole will see future students who also lack motivation and engagement in her career. She will also meet students whose personalities just do not gel with hers, creating tensions in her classroom.

So while this tension with that particular student might not be an issue, it is also not the last she will see of that tension. This is why it is so incredibly important for Nicole to be able to learn from this tension and how she managed it and grew from it. The next time that she might encounter a student that creates similar tensions, she will have new tools for supporting that student and moving past her tensions.

The same is true for tensions caused by interactions with staff and administration. Many times the tension is heightened due to its impact on their teaching, or ability to teach well. An example for this would be Paula's tension regarding teacher evaluation. The teacher evaluation process might not have anything to do with her students; however, she noted that the time that she spent on her teacher evaluation had her dividing her attention from focusing on her students.

She indicated staying up late, and worrying about it during her prep time, two ways that get in the way of her focusing on her students and the planning for her next lesson. The teacher evaluation system is not going away. Paula will always have something to do to document her efforts as an educator. And while she will work to lessen the tensions this school year, they will be back next year.

Depending on the class, the students' needs, and the time and effort she devotes to being a great educator, how she experiences this tension will change. She WILL have grown from experiencing the tension the previous year, but when she works with new students, these tensions will come up again. Or a variation of that tension. Paula will continue to need to complete the expectations for evaluation, but that is aside from her job responsibilities with the students. Based on the needs of those students, the energy that she has for extra tasks related to schools changes. This is why that tension will be back each year.

Another example would be tensions experienced by a teacher who was asked to be part of another committee. Ariel is a prime example of this. Ariel has been pegged for just about every committee that her school has had. Many of them align with her passions and strengths and drive to add to the school community. Others, however, are due to co-workers or administration reaching out asking her to be a part of them. Ariel, more often than not, agrees to help out. This does create added tension in Ariel's life.

Not only does she find herself out of her classroom more often, attending the meetings associated with those committees, but also she finds herself that much more pressed for time to meet with co-workers and students. She also very much noted her own personal tension of being an exceptional educator, and getting student feedback to them in a timely manner. Due to the sheer number of roles and meetings she has, this sometimes creates additional tensions in her life.

In each instance above, it should be noted that none of these examples of tensions will ever be alleviated. Versions of these tensions emerge every day. This is why it is so important to name them, learn from them, and grow professionally in how to handle them. In some of the cases, it is lessons on time management—understanding how to rebalance your time when there is quite a bit on your plate. For other times, it is learning to say no!

In education, this is not something that many teachers and administrators do often enough as each opportunity is always posed as being "for the good of the kids." This is very important to continue making the best decisions for the students as possible, but one of those decisions is also taking care of the teacher's mental health.

As previously noted, when teachers are experiencing increased levels of stress, their effectiveness in their classrooms decrease. Navigating a tension that involves someone having to say no is definitely uncomfortable, but also offers quite a bit of personal and professional growth. It also helps the educator understand their limits, while also being cognizant of the needs of others around them.

TENSION AS OMNIPRESENT

The previous section recognized how tension will always continue to be present in the educational environment due to the students constantly changing and creating similar, if not new tensions. While ever-changing students can be labeled as a cause for constant tension, the reality is that tensions are omnipresent, always present due to human nature.

Individuals are constantly experiencing multiple tensions at a time. Typically, the tensions that have the greatest impact are those that they have not experienced before, or those for which there is no foreseeable outcome. Educators have learned to prioritize their tensions: greater tensions that take up the majority of their energy and attention, and lesser tensions that end up getting "swept under the rug," ones that are deemed unnecessary compared to others.

However, after one of the greater tensions is alleviated, the next tension "in line," so to speak, becomes present or has a greater impact. Leo described this phenomenon by saying tensions are almost like a counterbalance to experiences: "We have one tension that weighs us down, and when that tension is no longer present, we have a new tension to take its place." The education working environment is never completely tension free.

Ultimately, educators are constantly working in an environment of overlapping tensions. For example, a teacher might be working on an email to a parent that creates quite a bit of tension in their lives. Then they have a tension come up with a colleague coming into their room upset. More often than not, the tension of the email takes a backseat to the immediate tension that needs to be addressed. Hopefully after the new tension is resolved, new skills have been developed, and the teacher has a new perspective towards the initial tension. This results in the managing of the tensions, again more effectively and with less stress.

Here is a moment where again it's important to be reminded that tensions are not all bad! Hearing a statement that educators are working in environments where there are overlapping tensions can be intimidating and anxiety-inducing. However, when they look at tensions as the opportunity to stretch their thinking, to grow in management strategies, then the idea of having overlapping tensions should not be as intimidating. Especially as one recognizes that each overlap will allow for a new understanding in handling the next tension.

Antony agreed that there are tensions constantly present. He says:

> I think the tension that is always present is wanting to do a good job by the students and teachers. The other tensions come and go all of the time. Some last longer than others. Eventually all others resolve themselves. But the tension or pressure to make sure the kids and teachers get what they need is always there.

Basically, Antony recognizes the undercurrent to education is tension. As expressed by Antony in this context, underpinning tension is not always a negative thing. Understanding that the tension to constantly be the best educator, meeting the needs of the students and the teachers, is inherently part of the job of education. This internal pressure to be the best is a great demonstration of tension as omnipresent, YET also manageable for educators to live with and understand. Again, the idea of constantly present tension is one that is nerve-racking, but not when one realizes that they have been doing it so far in their career. Now this text aims to simply give them a name.

TENSION PUSHES PEOPLE OUTSIDE OF THEIR COMFORT ZONES

This is one of the greatest benefits of tension, bar none. The fact that tension pushes people outside of their comfort zone is a positive effect. In the college classroom, for a teacher preparation program, one question that was asked to each semester's worth of students has been "What makes a great teacher?" and "What are the characteristics of your not-so-great teachers?"

Without fail, the response to the question regarding the not-so-great teachers relates to ideas such as "boring," "inflexible," and "route-work that is the same year-after-year." The teacher who hands out (or displays) the notes, then reads through the notes for the class, while you frantically take notes and try to absorb the material, is a teacher who fits all of these ideas and concepts.

This teacher, whose content rarely changes, who is not responsive to the knowledge or the needs of the students in front of them, is *most likely* a teacher who has not experienced tension and grown, changed, or been pushed outside of their comfort zone by it. Since so many feelings that are associated with tension are negative, it inherently pushes people beyond their comfort. It's outside of one's comfort zone that the greatest growth can occur.

This past year, the school years of 2019–2020 and 2020–2021 proved how living in tensions resulted in the entire educational system to move outside of their comfort zone, and the innovation and creativity that resulted from it are incredible.

TEACHING IN THE TENSION OF A GLOBAL PANDEMIC

By April of 2020, pretty much the entire educational system in the United States, if not across the world, was stalled. Schools were closed and quiet. Teachers and students were sent home. All educational content was being pushed out to students through a variety of distance learning options. For some this included through virtual platforms. For others, it was printed off/dropped off content. For some it was a complete stall and returned when things were safer.

No matter the structure that was adopted, every aspect of education was forced to reevaluate and restructure. Teachers needed to get creative with how they could deliver their content. They were pushed well beyond their comfort zones—many to a near breaking point. A study published in the *Journal of Pediatric Research* notes: "Teachers experienced on average a medium-to-high amount of stress during the lockdown" (Klapproth et al., 2020, p. 446).

The majority of this stress and tension comes from the use of technology to communicate their curriculum. This includes the learning curve of what they needed to do to master new technology, and the stress associated with student access. The tensions brought forward during this time were ones that the teachers had most likely never experienced. And yet, as the pandemic continued, and educational systems found themselves in a distinct learning format for longer, the teachers found ways to continue to be successful and meet the needs of their students.

The teachers managed this new tension. They found communities of support to be able to express concerns, garner ideas, and relate to the tensions brought forward. Social media platforms exploded with teacher communities, specifically focused on teaching during a pandemic. Technological platforms opened up free online training programs, and support programs for teachers.

Many paid platforms ceased their paid subscriptions in order to offer support to educators and families as they navigated this new normal in teaching. All of this growth and opportunity came from the tension that teachers experienced in pushing out their curriculum to their students.

While the tension experienced by many educators and families was uncomfortable and negative, there was incredible support and developments that became available to aid those groups through the tension. Many of these supportive programs and practices that were put in place during the pandemic are remaining in place as students return to schools and their classrooms. This will result in increased successful individualized learning opportunities for students, and support for their continued learning outside of the classroom.

This is just one additional concrete example of how tension encouraged change within the educational system. The educational system is poised for change due to the forced adjustments brought forward by the pandemic. Luckily, due to the management of those tensions, there are options to move forward with those changes.

ONE-SIZE-FITS-ALL MENTALITY

Occasionally, the school office will be filled with quite a few students waiting to see the principal. Some of the infractions are from behaviors that occurred on the playground, inappropriate comments to peers or teachers, illness, or not completing assigned work. This is one of the many responsibilities of a principal: to take care of and manage student behavior. As the principal tries to get to the underlying causes of behavior in the classroom, one common theme is that the student doesn't feeling connected to the academic content. Students will say, "I don't like to write," "I'm not good at math," and "I don't want to read that."

After many conversations, and perhaps many failed attempts of motivating the student, the principal and the teacher, exasperated, may throw their hands up and say, "Well, you may not like it, but sometimes you have to do things you don't like in life." This may be true, but it's hardly the motivation or inspiration a disengaged student needs to relight their fire.

The same is true for a teacher or administrator experiencing tensions. Hearing a statement like "You just need to do it" does not often do anything to alleviate tensions for the teacher or administrator and, oftentimes, creates a breakdown in purpose and understanding for them. Unfortunately, it is a statement that is heard quite often as new initiatives are being brought into the schools. Oftentimes these initiatives are district driven, but can also be administration driven. The concept of "just do it" is one that more often than not creates tensions.

Let's use JoAnne as an example. JoAnne is an excellent educator—she is hard working and has had multiple opportunities that have allowed her to grow professionally in her expertise in teaching. Now, JoAnne's school implements a school-wide book study on a topic that JoAnne had already intensely studied. Her excitement and motivation for participating in this book study is a bit lower than the rest of her team. Now, add in the fact that the district brings in experts to walk the group through this book study.

JoAnne believes that her knowledge on the topic is equal to if not greater than that of the expert brought in. This creates a tension for JoAnne. While many of the other teachers will benefit greatly from this study, it is not going to meet JoAnne's needs to participate here.

On the flip side, let's look at Matt. The exact same situation was presented to his team. Matt's school implemented a school-wide book as a Professional Learning Community (PLC) on a topic that Matt's team was more familiar with. Matt recognized that this was not in the best interest of his team and their time, so he went to his administrator and brought forward his concern.

Matt advocated for his team, and his administration was responsive and open to meeting the needs of their teachers. Therefore, Matt's team was allowed to use their PLC time to catch up on grading, team planning, and responding to parents, something Matt's team greatly needed and appreciated. This is a concrete example of meeting the needs of the teachers on this team. It also took Matt, as an experienced teacher, to speak up for the needs of the teachers and propose a solution to make things better.

Finally, let's take a look at Leo. As an administrator and school principal, Leo decided to invest time, funds, and commitment to his school, closely looking at racial tensions and challenges in the educational environment. Leo brought in speakers and opened up platforms for conversation around this topic for a full school year.

The very next year, the district decided to make racial justice the focus on all district professional developments across the schools. The district paid to have speakers come into each building. The work that Leo had started the previous year was beyond the conversations of where the new speakers were coming in. Instead of letting this create additional tension for Leo and his team, Leo reminded the group: "Race is something that should be talked about many times, in many capacities, hearing many different voices. Our work can always be improved on, or built up."

Leo also knew that he could take the conversations that the district speakers were starting, and build a bridge for his teachers, to meet them where they were at and match the work that they had already done.

Each of these examples represent the need to think of educational environments beyond the one-size-fits-all type of environment. Pushing beyond this type of thinking will benefit the students, the staff, and the administration in making a supportive, inclusive, and successful learning environment. We are constantly asking teachers to differentiate their instruction to meet the needs of their students, but we are not always looking at how we differentiate expectations to meet the needs of the teachers and administrators.

ONE SIZE FITS MOST

Buffets, add-your-toppings ice cream places, cafeteria lunches if the lunch ladies like you—those are places where one can get what they want, and there is a little bit of everything for anyone. No matter their tastes, preferences, or allergies, anybody should be able to find something that they will enjoy, and when everyone makes it back to the table, one can clearly hear the enjoyment in the meal from everyone, yet no one has the same looking plate.

SHOULDN'T SCHOOL BE LIKE THIS?

Just imagine, for a minute, teachers have their choice of entrees from the food bar, choices specifically laid out by the administrators in the school, sans grading expectations and the need to follow strict curricula. Teachers will flock to their favorites, maybe taking a bit of this to try, and loading too much of that. But the thing is, every teacher will have something on their plate, something to come back to the table with and share, and compare, and connect with others around them.

Compare this to the options and choices that teachers have in their professional development, in their learning, in their expectations in school. Imagine teachers who were not afraid of the reporting out on scores, driving their need for students to do the curriculum their way. What would the culture around school be like?

Going back to Matt's example from above—the fact that his administrator gave his team the flexibility to use the professional development time for something that was a need for his teachers showed responsive leadership that is flexible and adaptable to the needs of the staff. Matt's team was appreciative of the flexibility that was afforded to them by the administration, and productively used the time well.

This is not to say that all professional development opportunities should be optional. Understandably there are many initiatives that remain important for all teachers to experience. Considering the delivery of that professional development, and the school's background on the topic, is one way to lessen tensions surrounding professional development.

Are there ways to implement the initiative at varied levels, meeting the needs of the knowledge that the teachers have on the topics? Are there new and innovative platforms for that professional development? One thing that many have learned about teaching and working during a global pandemic is that there are many ways to deliver content and many ways to receive content. Teachers all over the world were finding new ways to differentiate their content to meet the needs of their students. It is fair to believe that districts can rethink some of their professional development practices and their delivery methods to meet the needs of their teachers.

Here comes our caveat.

The important thing with this will be to maintain the community and foster conversation around that professional development. Most professional development will be strengthened by the conversation that occurs afterwards. While technology allows for greater flexibility in the delivery, it also decreases the opportunities for genuine, in-person conversation.

Herein lies the struggle and the balance that we do not have the answer for, because that answer will come in response to your school's and your educational community's needs. This is not a concept that can be blanketed with a generic plan. Instead, the purpose of this conversation is to encourage additional thought here, recognizing the tension that comes with approaching professional development as a one-size-fits-all solution.

I STILL LOVE TEACHING

This is the simple truth. That while tensions have a major impact on the lives of educational professionals, they still show up, every day. Both figuratively and literally, showing up for their students, learning to live and work within the tensions to be better educators, to bring forth better practices, and to rise up to meet the challenges that arise because they love teaching. As Leo put it: "I am still learning every damn day, learning every day on how to do my job better because if you are not growing, you are dying."

TENSIONS DON'T IMPACT OUR CALLING

Being a teacher is much deeper than a profession—it's a vocation. As outlined by Buijs (2005) in their article "Teaching: Profession or Vocation?":

> To view teaching as a vocation, then, is to acknowledge a call to serve others through the means of education and learning, be it at a primary, secondary, or post-secondary level.... We do not merely choose teaching from among a range of alternative careers that may suit our personal interests. Rather, we assume a teaching role and whatever is involved in fulfilling it out of a sense of duty. The role itself, moreover, is directed toward others, because it is after all their learning that is the purpose of education. (p. 333)

As an administrator, Craig found he saw this in his teachers every day. He recognized: "I know that kids matter to you guys first. What you guys do is not a job, it's a calling." Something that his teachers found their purpose in, found their sense of duty towards, and in which lies their passions. And as an administrator he worked to bring out this sense of vocation in how he interacted with, and understands, his teachers. As a teacher, he knows that this is why he is in his profession—because he is called to be there for the students.

This is what allows the administrators and teachers to live and work in a space of tension. Because they know that the tensions that occur are part of the growth and learning that happens in education. That even in the space of tensions, their work with their students is what creates purpose for them. Paula simply stated: "I love my job. Absolutely love my job. I love my job, I mean I just work with the challenges." Challenges will always exist, but that does not take away from the love of what she does every single day.

Finally, Nicole also agrees with this idea—that the positives in her interactions with her students outweighs the negatives that are associated with the tensions of her profession. She says:

> Enjoyment for my job mostly comes from the students themselves. And when you've got a class that is gelling, and you can kind of really enjoy the lessons with them and enjoy how they interact with the lessons and each other—there's a lot of joy that comes from that.

For Nicole, who experiences tensions both internally and externally, she knows that those tensions mostly disappear when her students walk into her room. She allows her focus to be on the students in front of her, on the learning that is about to take place, on the conversations she has and the growth that she sees. She recognizes that these are the aspects of her job that she chooses to focus on in the moment—not the parent email that she needs to send, or the disgruntled colleague or administrator. It is the students. Plain and simple.

TENSIONS ARE MORE MANAGEABLE BECAUSE OF A COMMUNITY

Along with the focus of education as a vocation, and the priority being the students, tensions are also made better by the culture and community that surround the teachers. In the conversations with the teachers and administrators, many of them mention the camaraderie of their community, of their support system being in the building with them. For them, tensions are made manageable because of the conversations, and the joy that comes from watching others around them, learning from each other, and working through those tensions together.

Leo positions this joy in his job by recognizing the incredible educators around him. For him, this is what lessens the tensions that he is experiencing in work. He says: "I love my job. What I really enjoy is when I can just go in and sit in a classroom and watch a teacher teach. I am so in awe and appreciative of all the skills that they have."

While other aspects of Leo's role as an administrator are less glamorous, and quite a bit more tension filled, his ability to step back and step into his classrooms to just watch his teachers is a way that he refills his "metaphorical cup of joy," one that allows his focus to be on the positive rather than the negative associated with tensions.

In a similar manner, Matt appreciates the learning that takes place with his colleagues to lessen the tensions within education. In respect to his teachers being open to his community of learners he states: "I think they see the discussion, the openness, the conversation, the willingness to be vulnerable with colleagues, that kind of brings them on board and they understand this is a safe space"—one where they can work through tensions together.

A safe space for them to feel supported in the tensions they experience and know that "this too shall pass" in conjunction with the efforts of being part of something greater . . . that the teachers and administrators are all in the environment together, working through the needs of the students, the tensions and challenges of the day, for the greater purpose of loving their job.

This chapter focuses on the fact that educators are always living in a space with visible and invisible tensions. One of the first steps to living in tension is being able to name and understand that tension. It also showcases that this is okay, and that while we live in these tensions, we understand them, learn how to manage them, and grow because of them.

The chapter also highlighted two different ways that tensions have been addressed in the recent educational environments. It recognized the tensions that were created due to the coronavirus pandemic and how educators experienced that tension and grew from that tension. There are many educational support systems that emerged due to the pandemic that will continue to benefit educational environments moving forward.

Furthermore, the chapter looked at how professional development opportunities can grow and thrive due to the management of tensions. This includes differentiating those opportunities and meeting the teachers where they are at as it relates to the opportunity.

Finally, this chapter closed out by looking at how tensions do not impact a teacher's overall purpose of going into their profession—for their love of their jobs. Education is a vocation where individuals are called into a service to others. While tensions impact this service, returning to conversations as they relate to the students is where teachers find most joy and passion. Even though tensions negatively affect educators, the positivity of the classroom outweighs that negativity.

REFLECTIVE QUESTIONS

1. What are the tensions that are omnipresent in your educational environment?
2. What are the ways in which you have been pushed outside of your comfort zone through experiences with tensions?
3. What aspects of your educational job bring you the most joy and overshadow the tensions that you experience?

REFERENCES

Buijs, J. A. (2005). "Teaching: Profession or Vocation?" *Catholic Education: A Journal of Inquiry & Practice* 8(3): 326–345.

Klapproth, Florian, Lisa Federkeil, Franziska Heinschke, and Tanja Jungmann. (2020). "Teachers' Experiences of Stress and Their Coping Strategies during COVID-19 Induced Distance Teaching." *Journal of Pedagogical Research* 4(4): 444–452.

Plummer, Laura, Beliz Belgen Kaygisiz, Cymara Pessoa Kuehner, Shweta Gore, Rebecca Mercuro, Naseem Chatiwala, and Keshrie Naidoo. (2021). "Teaching

Online during the COVID-19 Pandemic: A Phenomenological Study of Physical Therapist Faculty in Brazil, Cyprus, and the United States." *Education Sciences*, 11(3): 130. https://doi.org/10.3390/educsci11030130.

Conclusion

This book began with the analogy of tensions being like resistance bands. Bands cause discomfort, but ultimately, if used correctly, this equipment is a useful tool that can be incorporated into any exercise routine. Looking at a resistance band's function as a cause and effect relationship helps explain its benefit—causing deliberate stretching of the band increases its effectiveness as human muscle fibers are engaged in the act and grow stronger.

You were challenged to look at the tensions you face in your life in a similar way. The tensions are the cause and the effect is how you react emotionally, physically, or socially to the stress. Most of the time humans try to avoid tension, but, what if, instead of ignoring or accepting the tensions you face, you used them to grow? Instead of letting a source of tension fester, what if you analyzed the origins, determined a possible solution, and then engaged in actions that could reduce the tension's power?

The four questions proposed in the introductory chapters included:

- How does one identify the root cause of tension in order to better deal with it?
- What if we address the emotions, feelings, and negative thoughts linked to the tensions in our lives and take charge of them?
- Would this act ultimately change how we view the tensions that impact us?
- Are there such things as positive tensions?

HOW DOES ONE IDENTIFY THE ROOT CAUSE OF TENSION?

Perhaps the first step in dealing with tensions is to realize that they will always exist. We did not do any sort of scale to measure the amount of tension caused by the main seven themes, but with potential stressors identified as the system, colleagues, workload, students, parents, expectations, and communication, there are a lot of variables teachers and administrators must contend with in the profession.

Identifying the tensions that are having an impact requires vulnerability in two parts. The first is to acknowledge the feelings associated with tension. Is there anger? Is sadness present? Does it feel hopeless? Understanding the why helps to prevent any rash decision-making or projection of emotions where they do not belong.

An additional level of vulnerability requires an individual to look at their own role in the situation. Are they an active participant in exacerbating the scenario? Are they bystanders who feel helpless? Is there gossiping among colleagues, family members, and friends who are also perpetuating the situation? While there are tensions that are not able to be settled, understanding how one feels about it and then reacting in proportion to the situation helps to subdue the tensions.

Self-analysis, talking with others, and exercising during stressful times helped the educators in this book get to the root cause of their sources of tension. Not all situations were able to be quelled, but even the act of identifying the tension and why it was stressful helped to make the tension more manageable than if it was left to its own design. If it was left unattended then it grew and impacted an individual's ability to do the job at hand.

WHAT IF WE ADDRESS THE TENSIONS IN OUR LIVES AND TAKE CHARGE OF THEM?

What if someone has the resistance band in hand and rather than use it, they just stare at it? They know it is going to help tone muscles and improve strength, but it has to be used in order for those things to happen. One has to stretch it around the thighs and actually do the squats in order to see and feel its benefits.

What happens when one is confronted daily, weekly, monthly, or even yearly, with a source of stress? Perhaps a person feels it in the stomach as butterflies. Maybe one's mind has created a scenario that literally makes the person feel sick. Does a person just sit in those feelings? What if facing those tensions, naming them, and then creating a plan of attack not only helps to reduce the power of the tension, but also promotes growth?

In this scenario, the tensions lose some of their control. Perhaps they do not give up all of their hold, but a person is in control of the reaction to the tension and thereby has greater power to choose the response. An educator may not agree with the systems in place within an academic setting, but rather than losing sleep, name the tension, figure out why the negative reaction is occurring, and then determine a course of action. It may not be the perfect course of action, but it helps if a person is in charge of the tension, instead of the tension taking charge of the person.

DOES ADDRESSING TENSIONS CHANGE HOW WE VIEW THE TENSIONS THAT IMPACT US?

If one does this, names the tension, figures out why the negative reaction is occurring, and determines a course of action, does this change how a person views tension? Many of the teachers interviewed intentionally changed the word *tension* to *challenges*. And in this sense negated the power of the tension from something that could not be overcome to now an issue that could be dealt with using stoicism and creative thinking.

Could this philosophy be used for all the themes the educators put forth in their interviews? Could issues with the system, colleagues, workload, students, parents, expectations, and communication be looked at as challenges that could be overcome with creative thinking?

Having a difficult conversation with a colleague is not easy, especially when there is the potential for a working or personal relationship to be damaged. But, what is the alternative? This is a prime example of vulnerability coming into play. Is the tension that is present impacting people's ability to do their jobs? Is it impacting students? If the answer to either of these is yes, then the difficult conversation needs to be had. Could the conversation come from a place of caring about the other person? Could the discussion be one of solidarity yet enhance the idea that at times there are items educators are required to do?

If the answer is no, that the tension is not impacting people's ability to do their jobs or impacting students, then perhaps some introspection is needed. Why is this a personal source of tension? Being honest with oneself about why the situation is a stressor is also part of personal growth. This process can uncover biases, tendencies, and perspectives that we may not have been aware of in our own minds.

Perhaps using the resistance band is not the best way to address a New Year's fitness goal. There could be any number of reasons that it might not be a good exercise to incorporate. It does not mean that fitness should be avoided altogether. Now, apply that perspective to tensions. Just because the first solution may not work does not mean the tension should be ignored. Additionally, because there may be no easy solution does not mean a tension should be ignored.

ARE THERE SUCH THINGS AS POSITIVE TENSIONS?

With all the negativity associated with the feelings and emotion brought on by tensions we look at the final question. Do positive tensions exist?

First, let's separate tensions into two distinct categories: those tensions that one chooses to take on versus those that are thrust upon a person. Tensions one chooses to take on may include those associated with a new leadership position, accepting a different academic role, or working with new colleagues. People take on these roles perhaps for better pay, new experiences, or enhanced learning opportunities. And while one may not know the direct tensions that could arise, being willing to take them on is a choice that a person makes.

The second category is those tensions that one does not select to take on, instead they are thrust upon a person for some reason. Examples of these could be: student behaviors in the classroom, being responsible for a new workload task, communicating new policies or initiatives, and finding oneself in disagreement with a system's direction, to name a few. These stressors can arise at any time and have the potential to impact one's ability to do the job at hand.

Tension is tension no matter how it is categorized, but do the different paths impact whether a tension is viewed as positive or negative? If one chooses to take on a tension, does that make it a positive? Does changing the term *tension* to *challenges* make it inherently more palatable? There are two sides to this argument, no and yes.

The term *tension* itself has negative connotations. If something were a positive tension it might invoke more positive phrasings, such as "butterflies in your stomach" or possibly even "a sense of excitement." In using the word *tensions*, no teachers or administrators here discussed their sources of stress using these more positive terms. Do they love their jobs? Yes. Are they looking out for the best interests of the students? Absolutely. Was each striving to reach various goals in their careers? In most cases, yes.

But, did they talk at all about the tensions as helping them reach their goals or make the profession more manageable? No. In fact, the tensions were holding them back from being their best selves, whether they were conflicted about directives or upset with colleagues. Therefore, the rationale for no is that tensions themselves cannot be positive even though the outcomes of facing those tensions may be beneficial.

On the flip side, there is the rationale that yes, tensions can be positive. The very act of facing the tensions is a form of positivity. It would be possible to duck one's head in the sand and ignore, but acknowledging and taking on the tension can be seen as a positive scenario because it demonstrates that the person wants to improve the situation. And, while negative feelings and emotions may arise during this time, it is a good thing that a person is willing to face the fire and move forward in order to possibly overcome the tension-filled situation. Finally, tensions promote growth, each and every time. Growth in education is always a positive thing.

It ultimately comes down to perspective. If a person has to do one hundred squats with a tension band and knows it is going to hurt, is the exercise itself viewed as positive or negative? Or, does the idea of it cause so much stress that the resistance band is continually put away for another day when, perhaps, it will be more tolerable? Just as there are multiple lenses with which to view each educator's story, there are also multiple lenses to view tension itself.

The hope is that this book has shown new ways to perceive the tensions that are impacting educators' abilities to do their jobs. Whether the stress lies in the themes of the system, colleagues, workload, students, parents, expectations, and communication, or is in a category not covered here, there are steps that can be taken to attempt to own the tension. Discover its source. Name it. Decide upon a course of action. It seems a simple enough strategy, but one that bears repeating every once in a while, especially when one is mired in a tension-filled situation.

Tables

Table 1.1 Examples of Tension   7

Table 1.2 Pseudonyms for the Educators Who Were Interviewed   11

Table 4.1 Principal Competency Skills versus Teacher Interview
  Category Alignment   62

About the Authors

Chelsea Faase, PhD, is a current professor of leadership, literacy, and social foundations at the University of Wisconsin–Oshkosh. Dr. Faase has spent twelve years in K–8 education, where she spent time teaching at the elementary level as well as middle school level. She taught general education at the elementary level, specifically fourth grade, and English language arts at the middle school level, collaborating in a co-teaching experience with special education educators. Chelsea obtained her PhD in urban education, specifically curriculum and instruction, from the University of Wisconsin–Milwaukee, where her main research focused on how teachers plan for and implement strategies that motivate adolescents to engage in literacy activities. Additional passions and research areas include children's and adolescent literature, the importance of inclusive text and culturally relevant pedagogy, and expanding the definition of literacy to meet the needs of all learners. Chelsea has presented at a variety of local, state, and national conferences on topics related to literacy. Topics covered include motivating adolescent literacy learners, differentiated learning K–12, gifted and talented literacy learning K–12, utilizing technology in the literacy classroom, and co-teaching with special education in a literacy classroom. Chelsea also consults with local schools and districts on their disciplinary literacy practices, as well as best practices for learning limitation students. Chelsea sits on a variety of local nonprofit boards of directors, specifically agencies that impact local youth.

Sheila Kohl, PhD, is a teacher in the School District of West De Pere located in De Pere, Wisconsin. She has taught a variety of subjects in her two decades as an educator, most recently teaching science and STEM. Dr. Kohl is a grade-level team leader, presenter, digital learning team member, teacher mentor, and educator effectiveness coach for her district. A former adjunct professor with Saint Mary's University of Minnesota, she is also a National Board certified teacher-middle childhood generalist, a *National Geographic* certified educator, has taken part as participant and critical friend for ASCD's Teach to Lead Initiative, and served as a content analyst for EdReports and as an edTPA assessor. Sheila is the recipient of the University of Wisconsin–Green Bay Distinguished Alumni Award, Herb Kohl Teacher Fellowship, Partners in Education Golden Apple Award, and was a finalist for both the Presidential Awards for Excellence in Math and Science Teaching and the National Teachers Hall of Fame. She has presented at numerous conferences, including ASCD Empower. Sheila earned a master's degree in applied leadership from the University of Wisconsin–Green Bay and a PhD in leadership from Marian University, specializing in teacher self-efficacy and teacher leadership.

Jason Lau, PhD, is the principal at Westwood Elementary School and Phantom Knight School of Opportunity, a project-based charter school, for the School District of West De Pere in De Pere, Wisconsin. He earned a master's degree in school psychology from the University of Wisconsin–Whitewater and a PhD in educational leadership and policy analysis from the University of Wisconsin–Madison.

Prior to becoming a principal, he served as a school psychologist for the Milwaukee Public School District and the School District of Kohler. Additionally, he was the director of student services for the School District of Kohler and the School District of West De Pere. His breadth of experiences has informed his current research interests and journey as an elementary school principal. He has served as part of the District Literacy Leadership Sig (DiLL) for the International Literacy Association (ILA). He has presented at several regional and national conferences on topics related to literacy leadership. His recently co-authored book, *The Literacy Leadership Guide for Principals: Reclaiming Teacher Joy and Autonomy*, examines literacy leadership practices for principals.

www.ingramcontent.com/pod-product-compliance
Lightning Source LLC
Chambersburg PA
CBHW020125240426
43673CB00038B/604